THE HOMECELL GROUP STUDY GUIDE
STUDY GUIDE
VOLUME I

PAUL Y. CHO
THE HOMECELL GROUP
STUDY GUIDE
VOLUME I

WORD PUBLISHING

WORD (UK) Ltd
Milton Keynes, England

WORD AUSTRALIA
Kilsyth, Victoria, Australia

STRUIK CHRISTIAN BOOKS (PTY) LTD
Maitland, South Africa

ALBY COMMERCIAL ENTERPRISES PTE LTD
Balmoral Road, Singapore

CHRISTIAN MARKETING NEW ZEALAND LTD
Havelock North, New Zealand

JENSCO LTD
Hong Kong

SALVATION BOOK CENTRE
Malaysia

THE HOMECELL GROUP STUDY GUIDE (VOLUME 1)

Copyright © Dr. Paul Y. Cho

First published in Korean.
This edition copyright © 1990, by Word (U.K.) Ltd.

ISBN 0–85009–338–4 (Australia ISBN 1–86258–114–2)

Scripture quotations unless otherwise stated are from *The Everyday Bible, New
Century Version*, copyright © 1987, 1988 by Word Publishing, Dallas, Texas.
Used by permission.

Typeset by Suripace Ltd., Milton Keynes.
Printed and bound in Great Britain for Word (U.K.) Ltd. by Richard Clay Ltd.,
Bungay.

90   91   92   93   /   10   9   8   7   6   5   4   3   2   1

PREFACE

After Jesus was resurrected, He gave the great commission;

"So go and make followers of all people in the world. Baptize them in the name of the Father and the Son and the Holy Spirit. Teach them to obey everything that I have told you. You can be sure that I will be with you always. I will continue with you until the end of the world." (Matt. 28:19-20)

Preaching and teaching the gospel should continue until the Church is lifted out of the world to meet the Lord in the clouds. For us, teaching is to understand rightly the work of God's creation, Jesus' crucifixion, and the Holy Spirit's continuous working among us so that we may prosper in all things and be in health, just as our soul prospers, and fulfil our duties as God's children. I praise God, our Father, that the Yoido Full Gospel Church has been taught this way. I praise God also that the Holy Spirit is moving upon our believers and we are experiencing the fivefold blessings through Jesus Christ: (1) forgiveness of sin, (2) fullness of the Holy Spirit, (3) the grace of healing, (4) blessings, and (5) the second coming of Jesus. We are also experiencing the threefold blessings of salvation: redemption of spirit, soul and body.

When you study *The Homecell Group Study Guide* volumes one to seven, as we do in the Yoido Full Gospel Church, you will be covering the entire contents of the Bible in a systematic manner in seven years.

One of the major characteristics of this book is that it is like building a house of faith with the Word of God on a firm foundation, on three pillars: our good God, my Saviour Jesus Christ, and my Comforter, the Holy Spirit. I trust you will meet our Heavenly Father, the triune God, as you study with this volume.

I pray that the grace and love of God our Father will rest upon the leaders and members of homecell groups everywhere in the world and on all who will gather every week to study God's Word and receive the fullness of the Holy Spirit.

Paul Yonggi Cho, Senior Pastor
Yoido Full Gospel Church
Seoul, Korea

CONTENTS

HOMECELL WORSHIP IN THE
YOIDO FULL GOSPEL CHURCH

Worship is offering to God, our Father, the sacrifice of praise and adoration. God has made us for this purpose and we believers live to praise and worship Him. When we worship the Lord He is exalted and He blesses us. We also enjoy a close fellowship among our brethren.

Worship can be adjusted according to each church's needs or emphasis, but for worship services to be their very best, we at the Yoido Full Gospel Church in Seoul, Korea observe the following order.

Order of Worship Service

Preparation of heart for the worship service

Blessing the Lord	Silent Prayer (optional)	6 minutes
	Leading Prayer	
	Apostle's Creed	
	Praise and Worship	
Bible Study	Message for Today from	45 minutes
	The Homecell Group	
	Study Guide	
	Prayer for Individual Needs	
Thanksgiving Offering	Receiving the Offering	3 minutes
	Prayer for Offering	
Fellowship	Introducing New Members	3 minutes
Closing	Closing Hymn	3 minutes
	The Lord's Prayer	

Total time: approximately 60 minutes

KEY POINTS FOR SUCCESSFUL OPERATION OF A HOMECELL

1. Effective Soul Winning

a) Have a yearning desire to win souls.

b) Choose a specific person that you are going to witness to about Jesus Christ.

c) Prepare beforehand with sufficient prayer for that soul to be won to Jesus Christ.

d) Establish some social contacts in advance before you witness.

e) Diagnose the immediate needs of that person.

f) Share other people's testimonies who overcame similar difficulties.

g) After that person accepts Jesus Christ, care for his or her spiritual growth for at least three months.

2. Prayer for Homecell Members (1 John 5:14-15)

a) Pray for the sick.

b) Pray for the solution of members' personal problems.

c) Pray for personal goals and desires in their lives.

d) Pray for the fullness of the Holy Spirit.

3. Effective Counselling for Your Members

a) Let your members talk as much as possible.

b) Direct their eyes from their own situation towards faith.

c) Give them fundamental directives on the basis of the Word of God.

d) Before you conclude counselling, always pray together.

e) Encourage them to confess a positive faith.

4. Points to Remember in Your Homecell Ministry

a) Always guard your members against wandering into false teachings.

b) Always avoid unproductive and unnecessary talk.

c) Always avoid financial transactions among your homecell members.

HOW TO USE THIS BOOK

1. For each lesson, the homecell leader, together with homecell members, should read aloud **today's scripture**.

2. Recite the **memory verse** together three or four times to memorize it for the day.

3. Understand clearly the **objectives** set out for today's message.

4. The **leading questions** should be asked by homecell leaders and members should reply. These opening questions and answers will help the members to understand the contents of today's message more easily.

5. Each **reference scripture** verse should be checked by all the members together, right on the spot.

6. After the message is given, discuss with the members each **closing question**.

7. Begin to apply God's Word for today to your daily life. The **application** box is for the members' daily application of the Word of God studied during the homecell meetings. *The Homecell Group Study Guide* is only beneficial when the members practise in their daily lives the truths they have studied and shared with each other and the ways they were able to apply and are applying the Word themselves.

8. Let us welcome the Holy Spirit and trust Him so that He may become the leader and teacher in the homecell worship service through the homecell.

GOD CREATED US

INTRODUCTION

The God we believe in is a good God. The first thing God did was to create the heavens and the earth and all things therein by His Word. After completing the creation of all things, God then made man to rule over the earth that He had created. God's purpose in creating man was to have communion and fellowship with him and to receive glory. To fulfil this purpose, God established the garden of Eden, a blessed place where man could live and meet with Him. To live happily with all the blessings was the only thing that man had to do there. His living in the garden had already been endowed by God. But the first man, Adam, and his wife Eve transgressed by surrendering themselves to Satan's temptation through the snake. Man was judged by God and was driven out of the garden, falling under the curse of death. Therefore, without the providence of our loving God's redemptive plan for us through Jesus Christ, we sinners would have been condemned forever and bound to suffer helplessly in the pit of eternal damnation.

God created us

1. The Purpose of Creation
2. The Order of Creation
3. The Creation of Man
4. The Creation of Eden
5. The Temptation and the Fall
6. The Judgement
7. The Foretelling of Salvation

THE PURPOSE OF
CREATION

1. **Today's Scripture**
   1 Corinthians 10:31-33
2. **Memory Verse**
   Isaiah 43:7
   Bring to me all the people who are mine. I made them for my glory. I formed them; I made them.
3. **Reference Scripture**
   Psalm 19:1-6
   Isaiah 45:18
4. **Objectives**
   a. Let us find out – God's purpose in creating all things and man.
       – the meaning of our living.
   b. Once we recognize that all things were created by God, let us proclaim this truth to the whole world!

LEADING QUESTIONS

> ### Christians should live for whose glory?
> (1 Corinthians 10:31)

> ### Who is "I" in today's scripture?
> (1 Corinthians 10:31-33)

> ### What should we offer to God as His children?
> (Isaiah 43:21)

TODAY'S MESSAGE

In the beginning God created the sky and the earth (Genesis 1:1). After He had created all things by His Word, God created human beings to take charge over them (Genesis 1:27). Evolutionists deny the idea of creation by God, but people today no longer pay attention to the fallacy of the theory of evolution.

There are things about God that people cannot see – his eternal power and all the things that make him God. But since the beginning of the world those things have been easy to understand. They are made clear by what God has made. So people have no excuse for the bad things they do. (Romans 1:20)

17

Why did God create all things? What is the purpose of His creation?

The Purpose of God's Creation of All Things

First, God created all things for man. This is clearly shown when we look into the order of the creation as follows:

1) **The mineral kingdom** – including the air or "firmament" (AV), the earth, the sea, and so forth.

2) **The vegetable kingdom** – that which can be rooted in the mineral world.

3) **The animal kingdom** – the vegetable kingdom that sustains the life of animals.

4) Then God created **man** to rule over all of His creation.

God's purpose in creation was to reveal Himself to man by creating a beautiful world for him and giving that created world to him to enjoy and to dominate. After He created the world, God especially provided the garden of Eden for man where there was no ruin, no hurt, no lack, but only abundance. Yet when Adam and Eve transgressed they were driven out of the garden and began to experience the curse and spiritual death. Later, God sent Jesus Christ to make atonement for man's sin so that all mankind could be born again through the blood of Jesus Christ. So, to save man, God provided the suffering of the cross in which His purpose of creation was fulfilled. Only those born of God through Jesus Christ can truly fulfil God's creation purpose (John 1:1-18, 1 Peter 1:3).

As we have shared, God created all things for man and though man sinned and was removed from the garden, to fulfil His purpose of creation, God sent Jesus Christ later to suffer on the cross to restore man's rightful place with God. Unbelievers trust all the imperfect and mortal things of the world that pass away with time, but we, who have found the purpose of God's creation through the grace of Jesus Christ, trust only our God, the Creator. King David confessed in Psalm 20:7:
> Some trust in chariots, others in horses. But we trust the Lord our God.

This good God pours out His grace and love unto those who trust Him only. God blesses with all things those who trust God, truly desire His kingdom and want to do His will (Matthew 6:33).

The Purpose of God's Creation of Man

Many people, especially middle-aged non-believers who have lived half of their days, are seized with fear, doubt and hopelessness as they still do not know the meaning of life. They have struggled day and night with many goals for a better life but even after having achieved those things they still cannot help but feel an emptiness with the question, "What is the real meaning of life after all?" Blessed is the man who has found the meaning and purpose of his life.

What is the purpose and meaning of the creation of man?
First, God created man for His glory (Isaiah 43:7).

When God created Adam, He wanted to receive glory through him. He wanted Adam to give worship, praise and glory to God for the blessings that had been bestowed on him.

It is the same today. The ultimate responsibility of man is to worship, praise and glorify God. The apostle Paul taught believers in Thessalonica:
> *Always be happy. Never stop praying. Give thanks whatever happens. That is what God wants for you in Christ Jesus.* (1 Thessalonians 5:16-18)

Therefore, whether we eat, drink or whatever we do, we should do all to the glory of God.

Second, God created man to manifest His glory through man.

Before Adam fell, he didn't need to worry about what to eat, what to wear, or where to sleep since his good God provided every need for him. Jesus Christ affirms too that all the needs of humanity are God's business but our priority is seeking His kingdom and doing what He wants (Matthew 6:31-33).

Therefore, we must give ourselves to God so that God can accomplish His will through our living and this will bring glory to God.

Third, God created man to share His love.

God is love (1 John 4:8). To love, there must be an object to love and God made man as His object of love. So our God, the God of love, created man to share His abundant love through fellowship and communion. Adam and Eve, however, disobeyed God and were cast out of the garden of Eden. They lost God's love. But God provided a way to restore man through the cross of Jesus so that man now can receive God's love and can have fellowship with God again through the Word of God.

Humanity was never meant to be empty creatures thrown out to the world aimlessly like some philosopher's jabber. Man has a definite purpose and reason to exist. That purpose and reason is to give worship, praise and glory to God who did not even spare His only Son to be crucified on the cross, so that He could restore us and bless us. Therefore let us be awakened to discover the love of God and live up to His desire to receive joy and glory through our worship and praise.

CLOSING QUESTIONS

> ### For whom did God create all things?
> (Find answer from today's message.)

> ### By whom were all things created?
> (Colossians 1:15-20, Hebrews 1:1-4)

> ### What makes people praise our Father in heaven when they see believers?
> (Matthew 5:16)

APPLICATION

1. Let us examine our present life and discuss with each other if we are truly living a life that glorifies our Heavenly Father or not.

2. Let us meditate on how Jesus Christ manifested the fact that God created man for His love.

THE ORDER OF
CREATION

1. **Today's Scripture**
   Genesis 1:1-31
2. **Memory Verse**
   Genesis 1:1
   In the beginning God created the sky and the earth.
3. **Reference Scripture**
   Psalm 104
   Hebrews 11:3
4. **Objectives**
   a. Let us know that all the worlds are created by the Word of God.
   b. Let us study each stage of God's creation and learn how it relates in parallel spiritual truths to our daily living in the Lord Jesus Christ.

LEADING QUESTIONS

> **What was the status of the earth in Genesis 1:2?**

> **In what order did God create all things?**
> (Genesis 1:3-31)

> **How did God feel about His creation?**
> (Genesis 1: 4, 10, 12, 18, 21, 25, 31)

TODAY'S MESSAGE

God Created All by His Word.

In the beginning God created the sky and the earth. (Genesis 1:1)

God is the Creator of all things. He created all things by His Word. The heavens and earth at the beginning had been judged because of Lucifer's rebellion, causing the earth to fall into deep darkness and chaos, but God by His authoritative words restored this chaotic earth. Only through His Word, God created the chaotic earth into the beautiful wonderful earth that we know today. The power of God's Word is infinite!

This "Word" found in the Bible is Jesus Christ.

> *Before the world began, there was the Word. The Word was with God, and the Word was God. He was with God in the beginning. All things were made through him. Nothing was made without him.* (John 1:1-3)

Jesus Christ is "the Word of God" that created all things, judged the world and redeemed the world, Who became a man and lived among us (John 1:1-14). He not only created the heaven and the earth and all things therein in the beginning, but He is still sustaining all of His creation by His Word. He is also our Jesus, our Saviour Who shed His blood on the cross to redeem us from our sin.

The Order of God's Creation

God's creation was divided into seven stages. By studying each stage of God's creation, we will be able to know more about our Creator God, and also know the kind of successful living that should be ours.

Stage 1 - the creation of light
Light was created first. It lighted the chaotic and dark earth. Spiritual enlightenment can illuminate the undeveloped, void and dark world of today. The Bible teaches us that this light is Jesus Christ (John 1:9).

Therefore, when we receive Jesus Christ into our hearts and are enlightened by His light, we also receive spiritual enlightenment in our lives that will dispel the darkness and void of our lives and homes.

Stage 2 - the creation of the firmament
Firmament (AV) means the air or sky. When God divided the waters, the sky came into view. When the sea of our insecurity and fears is divided, likewise our faith will burst out. Like the sky spread boundlessly above us, we too can have boundless miracle-producing faith in our hearts.

Stage 3 - the appearance of dry land
God spoke the Word and dry land appeared. Just as God let the dry

22

land appear first and made it produce all kinds of grass, herbs and trees abundantly, God's blessing will be manifested through abundant fruit-bearing in our lives, when we have received direction from the Lord and walk in obedience to fulfil His plan for us. Each fruit and vegetable grows from only one seed, yet each fruit and vegetable contains more than one seed, showing God's generosity and overflowing abundance to all of His children.

Stage 4 - the creation of the sun, moon and stars
God created the sun, the moon and the stars for signs of day and night, for the four seasons of the year and for dates. This teaches us God's value of time. There is an eternity, and every day that passes brings us one day closer to that eternity. To discern and work out all matters and obstacles of life wisely and successfully we must fully understand that we only pass this way once. We must take advantage of every opportunity to walk with God and fulfil His plan for our lives.

Stage 5 - the creation of all animals and birds after their kind
God created all living creatures according to their kind and blessed them to multiply. We do not have to think twice to realize each creature mates with its own kind, giving reassurance of a God Who had a divine plan for His infinite creation. We should be filled with a sense of affluence when we look at God's riches in the sky, the sea and the earth made for mankind. A sense of God's abundant blessing is absolutely necessary in achieving a successful and creative life.

Stage 6 - the creation of man
After everything was made beautiful and for man, then God made man and placed him in His beautiful world.

Man was made in God's image and likeness, which suggests man has the ability to know who his Maker is. And he will never have lasting peace and happiness until he is able to commune with his Maker. Man also has an infinite potential. Man is a creature that can be successful in the Lord God. We were also destined to become rulers, to rule over all things (Genesis 1:28). We are therefore to take an affirmative and positive attitude towards our life.

Stage 7 - rest
The finality of all creation was peace and rest. After the creation, God rested. After a day of work the "sign" of a night means God wants us to take time to rest. If anyone does not possess true peace and rest in his heart, his life is just meaningless. As we have discussed above, through application of the work of God's creation we can lead our daily lives experiencing the good will of our God.

The Results of God's Creation

We have just viewed God's creation in seven stages. There is nothing imperfect nor incomplete in God's creation. God is perfect and God is good, so is all of His creation. God saw that it was good when He completed each stage of creation. By saying that His creation was good, God Himself witnessed His completeness and the perfection of His creation.

All of these good creatures made good by God were cursed because of the sin of Adam and Eve (Genesis 3:17). But our loving God provided His redemptive plan to fulfil His good will. Through Jesus Christ's perfect redemptive sacrifice the cursed creation was delivered from the curse and man was restored back to his position as a steward over all things. God blesses us by declaring that if anyone belongs to Christ, he is made new (2 Corinthians 5:17).

CLOSING QUESTIONS

> ### How can we know and understand the world was made by God's command?
> (Hebrews 11:3)

> ### What is the earth full of?
> (Psalm 104:24)

> ### What shall we do for our Heavenly Father Who created the heaven, the earth and all things?
> (Psalm 136:1-9)

Now consider the application of this lesson which you will find on the next page.

APPLICATION

1. Share any personal experience which touched you when you saw the glory of God manifested in His creation.

2. Let us not forget that those things that we enjoy but unwittingly pass by in our lives are all from God's grace. Let us give thanks to our Heavenly Father for each one of them, for example, health, families, air, water and all the basics that sustain life.

3. What new point did you learn through today's lesson?

THE CREATION OF
MAN

1. **Today's Scripture**
   Genesis 1:26-28, 2:18-25
2. **Memory Verse**
   Genesis 2:7
   Then the Lord God took dust from the ground and formed man from it. The Lord breathed the breath of life into the man's nose. And the man become a living person.
3. **Reference Scripture**
   Psalm 8
   James 3:8-10
4. **Objectives**
   a. By studying the way God created man, let us learn how man is made in the image and likeness of God.
   b. Let us deeply ponder the true meaning of the "likeness of God" so that we will know the true value of a human being.
   c. By comparing man's status before and after the fall, let us see the lesson presented for our faith to grow.

LEADING QUESTIONS

> ### Of what material did God form man?
> (Genesis 2:7)

> ### What is the nature of God?
> (Genesis 1:27; Ephesians 4:24)

> ### Who are "we" in Genesis 1:26?

TODAY'S MESSAGE

How did man come to exist in this world? What is the origin of the human race? This has always been the fundamental query of man together with the question, "What am I living for?" Man has always striven to find the answer but no one has been capable of receiving or giving the answer to this ultimate question. We are given the answer only when God reveals it to us through His Word of truth. Let us study the Word of God and find out how we were made.

Man was Made in God's Image and Likeness

All things were created by the Word of God. When He commanded, *"Let there be light!"* light came. When God spoke, *"Let there be lights in the sky to separate day from night,"* it was done. All living creatures in the sea and the sky and all the grass and trees were created by the Word of God. It was only man that God did not create by His Word. On the sixth day of His creation, God took the dust of the ground, formed man by Himself and breathed life into his nostrils to make him a living soul in the image and likeness of Himself. Here the word "breathe" is "neshamah" in the Hebrew, meaning energy, breath, wind or spirit. Being made especially by God in this way, man was distinguished from the other creations. The "living soul" means especially the soul of man. Man's spirit and soul were born when God breathed life into his nostrils and that material body of dust became a fleshy body that was very much alive. Man was made in this special manner. He was also made to reign over everything in the earth created by God.

What is the "Likeness of God"?

As God is the Triune God, Father, Son and the Holy Spirit, man consists of spirit, soul and body. Each office of the trinity of God is different from the others and so are man's spirit, soul and body different from each other. In the beginning, before he fell, man's spirit, soul and body were in communion with God. So, his spirit dominated his soul (self-consciousness) and his soul dominated his flesh so that the flesh was totally subject to the spirit and soul of man.

How can we prove man is made after the image and likeness of God?

Let us now study briefly the five characteristics that prove his likeness to God.

1. **A spirit.** Man can have communion with God because he has God's spirit. God is a spiritual being. Man is also a spiritual being, which proves he is made after the likeness of God.

2. **A moral being.** As a moral being, man was made in the likeness of God. Man discerns good from evil in the light of ethics and the sense of morality that was put into his conscience. But in the animal world morality does not exist. God is good (Psalm 119:68). God is right (Psalm 33:4). God is perfect (Deuteronomy 32:4). These scripture verses tell us much about God's moral attributes. And the

fact that man is also a moral being proves that he is made in the likeness of God.

3. **A rational being.** Animals act on instinct while man acts on rationale. The fountain of man's rationale is called man's mind or soul which holds all of his intellectual faculties. Man without rationale is like an animal. God is also a God of knowledge and wisdom (Job 37:16, Romans 11:33). Because man was made in the likeness of God, he is able to develop God-given intellect and advance in the culture that he enjoys now.

4. **An eternal being.** Man is different from animals in that he will live eternally. That is why man's spirit is left with only one choice at the time of his physical death: whether he should live eternally in hell or eternally in heaven. Man's eternal living is one likeness of God.

5. **A being with power and dominion.** God created all things and He puts them under His control (1 Corinthians 15:27). When God created Adam in His likeness He also gave Adam authority to govern all things (Genesis 1:26, Psalm 8:6).

As we have studied, man was made in the likeness of God by divine counsel (Genesis 1:27), but after Adam sinned he lost fellowship with God. To redeem him God had to send His only Son to pay the ransom that God demanded for sin – death. And Jesus went to the cross to pay for the sins of all mankind. What was Adam like before he transgressed?

The State of Man Before the Fall

a. **He was sinless.** Adam did not know sickness, death, shame, the power to do evil and be evil (Genesis 3:14-19, 23-24). Because of his sins and the sins of succeeding generations, he reaped these and more. When we are born again through the blood of Jesus Christ, the sting of sickness and death will be removed for us.

b. **He had power and dominion.** Before the transgression, Adam ruled over the fish of the sea, the fowl of the air, the cattle, and over every creeping thing upon the earth as well as all the earth (Genesis 1:26, 2:15, 20). Adam's power of dominion was a creative power. He was able not only to keep all things on earth but also to improve them. When we become "new creatures" by believing in Jesus Christ, we can be restored to have the dominion over our circumstances and power in prayer to improve them too (Psalm 8:6; Ephesians 1:17).

c. **He was harmonious.** Before Adam rebelled against God, his life was a life of perfect harmony. First, he enjoyed harmony in the relationship of his spirit, soul and body. Second, he was in harmony with nature. Third, he had harmony and unity with Eve. And he could also speak directly with God.

When we are born again and become new creatures in Jesus Christ, we will be declared righteous as if we had never sinned, like the first Adam (Isaiah 1:18). We will have control over our circumstances, and all things on the earth related to our lives (Psalm 8:6), as well as enjoy a beautiful life filled with harmony.

CLOSING QUESTIONS

> ### After whose likeness did the apostle James say we are made?
> (James 3:9)

> ### Man is made in the likeness of God. What is the nature of God?
> (John 4:24)

> ### How does Ephesians 4:24 describe the "new person" who was made like God?

1. We are glorious creatures of God, made especially by His love. Therefore I urge you to confess to yourself every day, "To my Heavenly Father, I am an important person; therefore I am important."

2. We are made in God's image and likeness. Let us ask ourselves if we are living spiritual, moral and rational lives. Let us also discuss with each other whether we are really enjoying our eternal life and our power of control over our circumstances.

THE GARDEN OF
EDEN

1. **Today's Scripture**
   Genesis 2:8-15
2. **Memory Verse**
   Genesis 2:15
   > *The Lord God put the man in the garden of Eden to care for it and work for it.*
3. **Reference Scripture**
   Isaiah 51:3
4. **Objectives**
   a. Let us find out what blessings God has granted to man.
   b. By studying the garden of Eden that was whole and perfect, let us capture the true goal for our faith life.

LEADING QUESTIONS

Who planted the garden of Eden?
(Genesis 2:8)

What kind of trees did God plant in the garden? What were the two special trees?
(Genesis 2:9)

What was the first responsibility of the first man, Adam?
(Genesis 2:15)

TODAY'S MESSAGE

What was the state of the garden of Eden, that was given by God to the first man, Adam? What was Adam's life like in the garden?

Why did God place the tree of knowledge of good and evil in the garden of Eden?

What should a sinner do to restore all the abundant blessings of the garden in his own life?

The Meaning of the Four Rivers in Eden

The garden of Eden, made by God, was perfect and rich in every respect. Trees were pleasant to the sight and good for food. Water was sufficient from the rivers running in four directions and the land was rich with natural resources galore. Nothing was lacking for man to live there. The Greek version translated Eden as "paradise", meaning "garden of joy". Especially when we look at the literal meaning of the four rivers in Eden, we can see how good and wholesome our God is.

The name of the first river was "Pishon" flowing round the whole land of Havilah. The land produced gold, bdellium and onyx stone. God had provided abundant treasures in His garden. From the beginning, God gave treasures to man because He wanted him to live a life of abundance.

The second river was called "Gihon" which means "rise above". God wanted man, whom He made very specially in His likeness, to rise above all creatures and reign over them. Even today, God wants us to rise above any difficulty, get out of the bondage of sin and greed of the world through the merit of Jesus' blood and live in the kingdom of God.

The name of the third river was "Tigris". When the people of Israel were captive in Babylon, Daniel, the great servant of God, fasted and prayed by the side of the Tigris river where he received the great revelation from God about the last days (Daniel 10:1-9). Thus the Tigris river may symbolize our meeting place with God for fellowship with Him. God wanted to enjoy eternal fellowship with Adam and Eve.

The fourth river was "Euphrates" meaning "being great". Great civilizations have always risen in the vicinity of the Euphrates river. God desired the first man Adam to multiply and flourish.

The Tree of Knowledge of Good and Evil

God gave Adam all the abundance of the garden of Eden and blessed him with intelligence to operate it but gave him one commandment: "Do not eat of the tree of knowledge of good and evil." Why did God give Adam the tree of knowledge of good and evil in the first place and then order him not to eat of it?

First, that tree was given as the "measure" of Adam's obedience towards God. After God had bestowed upon Adam such inconceivably stupendous blessings, He gave him the smallest commandment of all: "Do not eat of the tree of knowledge of good and evil." That was truly a small request from God who gave Adam all things. Here, we can see God wants an obedient heart from us more than any other magnificent offerings (1 Samuel 15:22). God wanted faith and obedience from Adam, and to measure his willingness to obey God, the tree of knowledge of good and evil was placed in the garden. Today, the same yoke and burden that Jesus requires of us is as light as this tree of knowledge of good and evil was to Adam – that is our faith in and our obedience to Him. Without obedience there is no faith and without faith there is no obedience. This is the law of God's creation from the days of the garden of Eden.

Second, the tree of knowledge of good and evil shows that God gave Adam a free will and wanted him to use it. God does not want a mechanical obedience or faith from man because He is a very personal God. God wants us to seek Him with all our heart and with all our soul for He knows that the obedience that does not come from our heart is just an act or a lie. God planted the tree of knowledge of good and evil and wanted to see Adam obey Him because of Adam's "free will" desire to obey. This free will given to Adam was an absolute free will in that he could obey or disobey God's word. God so loves man that He gave this free will to man. Giving man a free will witnesses that God desired Adam's *willing* obedience and love towards Him, springing truly out of Adam's heart.

The Restoration of the Garden of Eden

Today, through the cross of Jesus Christ, we may restore the garden of Eden that our forefather Adam once lost. To repent of our sins and believe in Jesus Christ is to fill our hearts and our daily living with the first blessings of Eden so that we may prosper in all things and be in health, just as our spirit is quickened, and we are given life in the Lord more abundantly.

Just as four rivers flowed out of Eden, there should be springs of living water flowing out of our lives. These are the rivers of living water that Jesus promised (John 7:38). Whosoever believes in Jesus will experience the overflowing of the river Pishon, or "material blessings", the river Kihon, or "continuous growth", the river Tigris, or "communion and fellowship with God" and the river Euphrates, "a deeper and wider more meaningful life". Even today, God wants to give us back the garden of Eden through the power of the blood of Jesus Christ.

Where Jesus is, it is heaven; and where Jesus is, is also the garden of Eden. Therefore when we serve Jesus we have the kingdom of heaven and the garden of Eden.

By fulfilling our duty of obeying and following only Jesus Christ, we may restore the abundant blessings of the garden of Eden and enjoy an ever more blessed life in the Lord.

CLOSING QUESTIONS

> ### What did God give to us?
> (Deuteronomy 8:10)

> ### What do the four rivers in Eden symbolize in our lives?
> (Find the answer from today's message.)

> ### Through whom did we get back all the riches of the garden of Eden and come out of poverty and the curse?
> (2 Corinthians 8:9)

APPLICATION

1. Search your heart. Are you living in Eden, with its full and rich blessings, or not? Share your "Eden" experiences of God's blessings in your actual living.

2. Reflect on the meaning of the tree of knowledge of good and evil and examine yourself to see whether you obey God's commandments willingly or reluctantly.

THE TEMPTATION AND
THE FALL

1. **Today's Scripture**
   Genesis 3:1-7
2. **Memory Verse**
   1 John 2:16
   > *These are the evil things in the world: wanting things to please our sinful selves, wanting the sinful things we see, being too proud of the things we have. But none of these things come from the Father. All of them come from the world.*
3. **Reference Scripture**
   1 John 3:1-4
4. **Objectives**
   a. Let us remember Satan's nature and how he tempted Adam and Eve. We should always resist the devil in Jesus' name.
   b. We were dead in sin and separated from God. But God redeemed us through Jesus Christ. Let us renew our gratefulness for His redeeming grace.

LEADING QUESTIONS

> ### Which animal was the cleverest of all the animals made by God?
> (Genesis 3:1)

> ### How did Eve answer the snake's question?
> (Genesis 3:3)
> ### How did her answer differ from God's command?
> (Genesis 2:16-17)

> ### What were the consequences of eating the fruit of the tree of knowledge of good and evil?

TODAY'S MESSAGE

God established a covenant with man whom He made in His likeness. God gave him the words of both blessing and warning simultaneously. If he obeyed, God would bless him, but if he disobeyed, God would punish him. Adam, tempted by

Satan, chose not to keep the command so he broke it. We will now study Satan's temptation and how Adam fell.

Satan's Cunning Temptation

Satan was a cherub angel in heaven but he disobeyed and rebelled against God, and he was cast out of heaven. Seeing Adam and Eve were enjoying communion and fellowship with God, Satan tempted Eve through the snake in a plan to separate Adam and Eve from God. There are reasons why Satan enticed Eve instead of Adam.

First, Eve did not hear directly from God about the command forbidding them to eat the fruit. God directly and firmly commanded Adam:

> *"You must not eat the fruit from the tree which gives the knowledge of good and evil. If you ever eat fruit from that tree you will die!"* (Genesis 2:17)

Eve was told indirectly of this commandment from God, so it was easier for her to doubt what God had said. It is the same in our faith life. When a person has no direct personal experience with God, but he is reluctantly attending church under pressure from his family members or neighbours, he will, like Eve, easily succumb to Satan's temptation.

Second, Eve was taking possession of Adam's heart. On this account, Satan approached and lured Eve whom Adam loved most. Even today Satan is always slyly tempting us to fall into sin through those we love most or the thing that we are concerned about the most.

Three Doubts that Satan Imparted

Before God, it is a grave sin for man to talk with Satan about God's absolute command which was not to eat the fruit of the tree of knowledge of good and evil. God's absolute authority should never become the object of man's dispute. As far as the question of our faith is concerned, there is no place for argument on our part. Before God, there is only absolute obedience or absolute disobedience to any of His commands. But Satan raised three doubts in Eve.

The first was the doubt about God's goodness. Satan said, (AV) *"...your eyes shall be opened."* This made Eve think God was hiding something better from them. Dissatisfaction was aroused in Eve's mind, and that led her to disobey God.

Second, Satan caused Eve to doubt God's truthfulness:

"Did God really say that you must not eat fruit from any tree in the garden?" (Genesis 3:1)

Satan deviated from God's word by saying *"You will not die"*, but God had clearly stated, *"You will die"*.

Third, Satan instilled doubt into Eve about God's holiness. Satan made Eve think that God had forbidden the fruit because of His jealousy that man would become like God if he ate the fruit.

Once these doubts formed in Eve's heart through Satan's temptation, the fruit of the tree of knowledge of good and evil (the symbol of God's absolute authority) began to be an object of lust to her eyes. From that moment of doubt, the fruit began to look so appetizing, so pleasant to the eye, and also so desirable to give her wisdom. Eve's heart had been full of obedience, faith, orderliness and harmony, but when doubt entered her heart, she began to see the fruit as an object of her lust of the flesh, her lust of the eyes, and her pride of life (1 John 2:16 (AV)). Finally, Eve touched the fruit, picked the fruit and ate it, and she lost the blessing of obedience. That same Satan who so cunningly deceived Eve is today tempting all of us by whispering, "Did God really say that?" When Satan comes so slyly and asks the same question of you and me, let us recognize it is Satan. Let us bind him in the name of Jesus Christ and preserve our soul by crucifying our lust of the flesh.

Man, After Eating the Forbidden Fruit

At the moment Adam and Eve ate the fruit of the tree of knowledge of good and evil against God's sovereign command, they not only lost their spiritual life but they also lost their moral and rational power, and fell under judgement in the midst of fear and disgrace. What were the consequences of their disobedience?

First, a sense of guilt, shame and fear smouldered in them. When sin came and their spirit died, they were separated from God eternally. Destruction followed in their human relationship too and also in the relationship between man and nature. Where this is sin, there is separation. Where there is separation there comes death.

Second, Adam and Eve, having eaten of the fruit of knowledge of good and evil, now became servants of Satan. To eat of that fruit of the tree of knowledge of good and evil is to break the law. And sin is breaking the law (1 John 3:4). The Bible declares sin is of the devil (1 John 3:8). Sin and the devil are inseparably related to each other. Fallen Adam, separated from God, now became one with the devil and under the ownership and power of the devil.

By eating of the fruit, Adam and Eve fell and their fall was a complete fall. Their spiritual, mental and moral character was totally altered and polluted. They also lost the faculty of discerning good and evil (Isaiah 5:20). Because of this total fall, they became separated from God and forsaken by God.

The fall of Adam and Eve was a total fall which influenced every aspect of man. Because all men are guilty of sin through Adam's transgression (Romans 3:9), no one can save himself by his own self-effort or any virtuous acts of hard training. On the side of mankind, the fall of Adam brought absolute despair.

All of these miseries were caused by our first parents' disobedience to God. It was because of their hurried engrossment in seeking self-interest instead of seeking God's interest, which is the glory of God. Because of their greediness they obtained the opposite of what they actually wanted to get. They fell into degradation, guilt, and punishment. Until mankind accepts salvation through the grace of Jesus' cross, it is doomed to remain in absolute despair.

CLOSING QUESTIONS

What was the result of Adam's transgression for the human race?
(Romans 5:12, 6:23)

What did Satan instil in Eve?
(Find answer from today's message.)

APPLICATION

1. Let us see how Jesus Christ resisted the devil's temptation and how we can apply His method in our lives (Matthew 4:1-11).

2. Satan attacks through our weak areas. By inwardly digesting the Word of God and praying diligently we can hold fast to our faith.

THE
JUDGEMENT

1. **Today's Scripture**
   Genesis 3:8-24
2. **Memory Verse**
   Romans 6:23
   > *When someone sins, he earns what sin pays – death. But God gives us a free gift – life forever in Christ Jesus our Lord.*
3. **Reference Scripture**
   Romans 5:16
   1 Timothy 5:24
4. **Objectives**
   a. Sin brings judgement. Let us avoid sin at any cost.
   b. The wages of sin can only be paid by the precious blood of Jesus Christ. Let us always give thanks to Jesus Christ Who paid this debt on our behalf by His redeeming grace.
   c. Let us perceive what is God's righteous punishment for sin.

LEADING QUESTIONS

> ### What did God ask Adam after he sinned?
> (Genesis 3:9)

> ### What was God's punishment for the snake, Satan?
> (Genesis 3:14-15)

> ### What will happen to the flesh of man when he dies?
> (Genesis 3:19)

TODAY'S MESSAGE

We have learned in the previous lesson how our first parents Adam and Eve were tempted by Satan, broke God's command and transgressed. Every transgression will inevitably be punished (1 Timothy 5:24). Adam and Eve were judged for their transgression. The snake which tempted Eve was judged too.

Man's Responsibility for Sin

Many people ask why man should be accountable for the sin when actually Satan induced man to fall into sin. But the Bible clearly shows that the liability for sin lies in man (Romans 3:23, 6:23).

Adam and Eve, by misusing their God-given free will, obeyed Satan instead of obeying God. God did not tempt them but they left God and were tempted by their own wills. Of course God, according to His good will, allows us to be tested for our growth but He never tempts us with evil (James 1:13).

There are two kinds of temptations: one, in the Greek language "peirazo", which is given by Satan, and the other, "dokimazo", which is the test coming from God through which our faith in Him grows one step further. While the test of "dokimazo" brings us more abundant grace and blessing from God, the "peirazo" from the devil only hurts and seriously mauls us.

Being tempted with evil (peirazo), and dragged along in improper desires, Adam and Eve gave birth to all sin. All sin inevitably demands that man pay its price. The verdict was eternal damnation and in no way was man free from the consequences – the burden of punishment.

However, our merciful God provided the way of redemption for us, as is evident through the animal sacrifices for sin in the Old Testament. As for us today, we can receive the grace of redemption by repenting of our sins and accepting Jesus because He died on the cross bearing all the sins of mankind.

The Judgement of God

God loved man and established a covenant with him, but man broke the covenant and fell into sin. Accordingly, God Who is righteous had to judge the sinner – the snake, the woman, Adam and also the creatures on earth. Let us see how each one was judged by God.

a. Judgement for the snake
The snake, a vehicle used by Satan in tempting man, received the most severe punishment from God. Though the snake was merely used as a tool by Satan, it was judged most harshly because the snake symbolized all evil forces. Look at the verses in Genesis 3:14-15 about God's judgement for the snake.

> *The Lord God said to the snake, "Because you did this, a curse will be put on you. You will be cursed more than any tame*

animal or wild animal. You will crawl on your stomach, and
you will eat dust all the days of your life. I will make you and
the woman enemies to each other. Your descendants and her
descendants will be enemies. Her child will crush your head.
And you will bite his heel."

Here we can see how much God hates sin, so that He cursed Satan, the mastermind of the snake's work. Jesus Christ, God's redemptive and gracious plan for us through the descendants of woman, now became the only hope left to all mankind.

b. Judgement for the woman

Then God said to the woman, "I will cause you to have much
trouble when you are pregnant. And when you give birth to
children, you will have great pain. You will greatly desire your
husband, but he will rule over you." (Genesis 3:16)

Through this verse, we can perceive that originally the pain of conception and delivery in childbirth was not meant to be so severe for women, but after Eve's sin, conception and delivery would be accompanied by pain and danger, with risk even to life. Not only this, but as a consequence of her sin, women were sentenced to lead a life forever pining for man's affection and always to rely upon man.

c. Judgement for Adam

Then God said to the man, "You listened to what your wife
said. And you ate fruit from the tree that I commanded you not
to eat from. So I will put a curse on the ground. You will have
to work very hard for food. In pain you will eat its food all the
days of your life. The ground will produce thorns and weeds
for you. And you will eat the plants of the field. You will sweat
and work hard for your food. Later you will return to the
ground because you were taken from it. You are dust. And
when you die, you will return to the dust." (Genesis 3:17-19)

God imposed the punishment of the curse and death on Adam who disobeyed God. When Adam's spirit prospered, everything was going well and his body was healthy (3 John 1:2). When Adam's spirit died, all of life became entangled with a struggle, in sweat, thistles, and thorns. Sicknesses and disease swallowed his health, eventually dragging him to death. If man is to be delivered from the curse, his spirit must first be born again and stand right before God.

d. Judgement for nature

Then God said to the man, "You listened to what your wife
said. And you ate fruit from the tree that I commanded you
not to eat from. So I will put a curse on the ground. You will
have to work very hard for food. In pain you will eat its food

all the days of your life. The ground will produce thorns and weeds for you. And you will eat the plants of the field." (Genesis 3:17-18)

Adam and Eve had been the master of their circumstances, ruling over them. When they fell, they also lost the mastery over those circumstances and they were judged. All the things under their rule were judged too. As a result, the fruitful soil of the earth changed to become a barren land. The land previously covered with beautiful fruit-bearing trees was now clothed with thorns and thistles.

Through one man's sin, his circumstances and land were cursed and the whole world is still suffering. Since then, everything God made has been waiting to be set free from ruin, as Paul said in Romans 8:18-23.

Our God judged the transgressors with His justice. The judgement was manifested as punishment. God not only judged man but also provided His redemptive plan to deliver him from transgression, judgement and death.

CLOSING QUESTIONS

> ### In just one word, what is the consequence of sin?
> (Romans 6:23)

> ### When you live the way the world lives, who are you trying to please?
> (Ephesians 2:2-3)

> ### What is the one and only hope now left for mankind?
> (John 3:16, Galatians 5:5)

APPLICATION

1. God is a good God but He is also a God of righteousness. Let us share with each other how we were corrected by Him when we stubbornly insisted on walking our own way.

2. Let us reflect seriously – why should the sinless Jesus hang on the cross?

THE FORETELLING OF
SALVATION

1. **Today's Scripture**
   Ephesians 2:1-10
2. **Memory Verse**
   Genesis 3:15
   > *"I will make you and the woman enemies to each other. Your descendants and her descendants will be enemies. Her child will crush your head. And you will bite his heel."*
3. **Reference Scripture**
   Luke 1:69-71
4. **Objectives**
   a. Let us remember our God is a God of love as well as a God of righteousness.
   b. Let us perceive the fact that when we believe in Jesus Christ we may also be restored to enjoy the blessings of the garden of Eden that were once lost by Adam and Eve's sin.
   c. Let us trust our God who promised redemption for all of us and has fulfilled His promise.

LEADING QUESTIONS

> ### What kind of God are we trusting?
> (Ephesians 2:4-5)

> ### How did we live before we believed in Jesus Christ?
> (Ephesians 2:2-3)

TODAY'S MESSAGE

In the previous lessons, we have studied the purpose of God's creation; the creation of the universe and of man; the blessings of the garden of Eden; the temptation of Satan and man's fall, followed by the judgement of God.

In this lesson, we shall examine the love of our God through the indication of His redemption plan to Adam and Eve, even though they transgressed and were judged.

God's Love is Eternal Love

God made man to share His love after He created the heavens and the earth and everything in them. But Adam and Eve transgressed by disobeying God, and hid themselves from the face of God among the trees in the garden.

But God, rich in mercy, visited Adam and Eve who had transgressed, and asked them, *"Where are you?"* Because of His love, God suffered too; He tolerated and called them AGAIN even though He could have destroyed them as the price of their sin (Genesis 3:7-12).

Even today, God still visits us who are dead in sin and calls our names. Since God hates sin, He could have destroyed all of us sinners right on the spot, yet inasmuch as His love is eternal love He is still calling us through Jesus Christ.

God also made coats from the skins of the animals and clothed Adam and Eve. The sinless animals, who were killed to provide a covering for the shame of the transgressors, provide a picture of the future death of Jesus Christ, the only begotten Son of God.

> *One man sinned, and so death ruled all people because of that one man. But now some people accept God's full grace and the great gift of being made right with him. They will surely have true life and rule through the one man, Jesus Christ.* (Romans 5:17)

The Flaming Sword and The Tree of Life

When Adam and Eve had to leave the garden of Eden after their transgression, God placed angels there and a flaming sword which flashed around in every direction. It was to keep Adam and Eve away from the tree of life, rather than to destroy the garden.

This fact shows that God intended to return to us, eventually, the blessing of the garden and the tree of life. In reality, God allowed us through Jesus' sacrificial death to have the power of eternal life, which is the fruit of the tree of life, as well as the enjoyment of the abundance in the garden of Eden.

Judgement always follows sin and in judgement there is always punishment. The sinner deserves and should receive judgement and punishment. Yet God did not throw us away to the wrath of judgement and dire punishment, but rather He determined to save us from these. His redemption was fulfilled at the cross by His only Son, Jesus Christ. Anyone who believes in Him will be saved and will receive forgiveness and peace with God.

We should give thanks to God that we are able to be under the cross of Calvary. In Jesus, Who died on the cross, is forgiveness of our sins, redemption of punishment, and we are blessed through His death. We can enjoy our redeemed life abundantly.

The Prophecy about Christ's Redemption

The Bible records the foreshadow of God's redemptive plan right after man fell and sinned. In Genesis 3:15 God said that the woman's descendant, or child, would bruise the snake's head. Here, the child means Jesus Christ, as He was conceived in a woman by the Holy Spirit (Luke1:30-35).

As we have seen so far, God's covering of Adam and Eve, who were full of consternation and shame after the transgression, shows symbolically the coming death of Jesus Christ, our Passover Lamb, to forgive our sins and cover our iniquities.

God also indicated redemption through the blessing He bestowed upon Abraham. The blessing that is flowing to all believers through Abraham is above all the blessing of salvation – being justified through faith – that made Abraham the forefather and the blessing of all believers.

God not only promised salvation to our first parents and Abraham, but through the mouth of His servant-prophets He also wrote the promise in the Bible in full. All of these prophets foretold that the promised redemption would be fulfilled through the Messiah (Isaiah 53:4-7). This promise was also given to the Gentiles. All the faithful servants of God in the Old Testament days longed for His coming.

As promised in His Word, God sent Jesus Christ into this earth, conceived by the virgin Mary. Jesus became the sacrifice for the salvation of all the human race by allowing Himself to pay the price of sin. His torn flesh became the bread of our eternal life. He shed His blood so that our sins are forgiven and we are declared righteous, and we have become kings eternally. Jesus is the source of our salvation.

This salvation is manifested to all people by the grace of God. When anyone believes in Jesus he can receive salvation. The Bible shows God's redemptive plan and its fulfilment in precise detail. Therefore, whoever hears Christ's words, believes in them with his heart and confesses with his mouth, receives salvation and is led to the abundant blessings of God. Let us be reminded again of the love of God calling us and give thanks to Him always.

They were shouting in a loud voice, "Salvation belongs to our God, who sits on the throne, and to the Lamb." (Revelation 7:10)

CLOSING QUESTIONS

What had been ruling people since the transgression of Adam and Eve?
(Romans 5:17)

What does the name "Jesus" mean?
(Matthew 1:21)

APPLICATION

1. When your heart is troubled, you are faced with many problems or your body is sick, think of the blood of Jesus on the cross, and be thankful that He paid the price for your redemption which includes your salvation from your sickness or problems.

2. Confess the following statement: "My being saved was ordained by God before the ages. I am a very important child to my Heavenly Father, He had chosen me and recognizes me as His child."

WE LEFT GOD

INTRODUCTION

One of the most miserable sights in the world is a man who has departed from God.

Through the transgression of our first parents Adam and Eve, all mankind was born in sin and not one single person has been capable of living without committing sin. In the Bible, the power of the sinful influence which descended from Adam is manifested in the homicide committed by Cain and his children and others. The moral corruption leading to the destruction of Sodom and Gomorrah reveals to us the worst state of mankind. Eventually, the spiritual ruin of Adam's offspring, which resulted in idol worship, fanned the flame of God's anger.

By studying the cases of these representative sins and sinners in Old Testament days, the lessons in this unit will deal with two important questions:

1. What kind of sin makes our Heavenly Father sorrowful?

2. What is the destiny of this sinful human race?

These lessons will help all of us to live a sanctified life which resists sin, and further provides a powerful witness to Jesus Christ for our unbelieving neighbours and friends.

We Left God

 8. The Original Sin and Subsequent Sin
 9. Cain, the First Murderer and Abel, the First Martyr
10. The Three Sons of Noah
11. The Builders of the Tower of Babel
12. Sodom and Gomorrah
13. The Poisonous Snakes and the Bronze Snake
14. The Disobedient King Saul
15. God-grieving Sins
16. The Consequences of Man's Fall

THE ORIGINAL SIN AND SUBSEQUENT SIN

1. **Today's Scripture**
   1 John 3:1-12
2. **Memory Verse**
   John 16:9
   > *"He will prove to them about sin, because they don't believe in me."*
3. **Reference Scripture**
   Romans 1:18-32
4. **Objectives**
   a. Let us recognize that all of us are sinners before God.
   b. Let us find out where sin originated and what its nature is, and let us depart from sinful living.
   c. Let us have a true knowledge of God. He is a holy God Who hates sin.

LEADING QUESTIONS

> ### What shows the extent of God's love for us?
> (1 John 3:1)

> ### What hope should we believers hold to?
> (1 John 3:2-3)

> ### What is sin?
> (1 John 3:4)

TODAY'S MESSAGE

Is there anyone on earth who has no sin at all? Is it possible that somewhere there exists a person who always thinks of good and does the right things all the time? The Bible steadfastly rejects this possibility.

> *As the Scriptures say: "There is no one without sin. None! There is no one who understands. There is no one who looks to God for help. All have turned away. Together, everyone has become evil. None of them does anything good."*
> (Romans 3:10-12)

The Original-sin-binding Posterity of Adam

All people in this world are born sinners. What made all of us, without exception, become sinners? Adam and Eve disobeyed God, ate the fruit of the tree of knowledge of good and evil and were cast out from the garden of Eden. Since then, Adam's spirit died and the blood of disobedience began to flow through him and also through his descendants who were born in the likeness and image of Adam (Genesis 5:3). Consequently, the sin of Adam's disobedience was handed down the lineage of all his offspring, the human race. Perceiving this tragedy, the Psalmist lamented:

> I was brought into this world in sin. In sin my mother gave birth to me. (Psalm 51:5)

This is what we call **original sin**. This original sin entered all of us through the first man Adam and we, for the wages of the original sin, are placed under the same judgement that Adam received in the beginning. Therefore, without the cross of Jesus Christ, no one single person can escape from the consequence of this original sin. Regardless of higher education, or a rigorous discipline of the mind for virtuous and ethical living, or a fair and perfect social system if there could be one, no one can run away from the bondage of original sin.

> Sin came into the world because of what man did. And with sin came death. And this is why all men must die – because all men sinned. (Romans 5:12)

The original sin that came to this world through the first man Adam was especially the sin of pride before the presence of God – that is, the human conception that people can also become like God when they develop and practise the ability and power to make a better environment to live in. Being born of original sin like this, humanity has been unceasingly rebelling against God and always building the "towers of Babel" of human pride.

Subsequent Sins

Sin is called "hamartia" in the Greek language, meaning "an arrow misses its target". Likewise, by doing a deed that missed the Word of God, Adam transgressed and became Satan-centred and also self-centred. Upon this all kinds of **subsequent sins** began to mushroom, based on his selfishness.

Subsequent sins always have their roots in original sin. The once-missed arrows of obedience and faith are actually planting small and big sins in our daily lives, like a cancer in the bloodstream proliferating malignant cells here and there.

We have just reviewed the close, inseparable relationship of original sin and subsequent sins. Such major sins are listed in Romans 1:28-32 and all people deserve God's anger on account of these sins.

Our sins are not merely a matter of ethics and morality. They have a deeper meaning, in that where there is sin there is always Satan, and where Satan is, there is always sin. Therefore when a person commits a sin in his daily living, he is confirmed a servant of sin because committing sin is just obeying Satan.

> *Surely you know that when you give yourselves like slaves to obey someone, then you are really slaves of that person. The person you obey is your master. You can follow sin, or obey God. Sin brings spiritual death. But obeying God makes you right with him.* (Romans 6:16)

God declares He will not listen to our prayer when we commit sins:

> *"You will raise your arms in prayer to me. But I will refuse to look at you. Even if you say many prayers, I will not listen to you. It is because your hands are full of blood."* (Isaiah 1:15)

However, we have been forgiven of original sin once and for all through the death of Jesus Christ on the cross, simply by asking for God's forgiveness; but for those subsequent sins committed after we were saved, the way of forgiveness is opened for us so that we can be forgiven when we repent of these sins and confess them to the Lord. Therefore, man has been forgiven of Adam's original sin, since Jesus paid the debt of the sin by His death on the cross, and those who have accepted Jesus Christ are no longer under original sin.

The Nature of Sin and Our Attitude Towards Sin

What is the nature of original sin and subsequent sins? How can we resist sin?

First, sin never leaves a sinner. Sin clings to a sinner, following after him everywhere, never leaving him alone. Sin is only removed by the blood of Jesus Christ.

Second, sin grows. There is an old Korean saying, "a thief of a needle becomes a thief of an ox." Small sins grow to become larger sins or increase on a bigger scale.

Third, sin separates man from God. Sin becomes a wall separating God and sinners. It cuts off man's communion and fellowship with God, and also the road which leads to blessing.

Fourth, sin eventually leads man to destruction. Sin makes man fall short of the glory of God (Romans 3:23), finally leading him to death, the eternal punishment (Romans 6:23).

Sin is evil and miserable. For this reason people with a true knowledge of sin struggle against sin even to the shedding of blood so that they may not wilfully commit any sin (Hebrew 12:4). But if we sin we should immediately repent, confess our sins to our Heavenly Father and seek His forgiveness (1 John 1:9).

Most of all, to keep ourselves from sin every day, we must always pray to our Lord, "Our Father which art in heaven, Hallowed be thy name .... but deliver us from evil." As long as we pray this prayer with all earnestness and think on our Father's holy name, obeying His Word fervently so that His name will be hallowed through our daily lives, we will not sin wilfully and the sin-bringing Satan will be defeated before us.

CLOSING QUESTIONS

> ### What do we make God to be when we say we have not sinned?
> (1 John 1:10)

> ### What is the reason that prayers do not reach our Heavenly Father or are not answered by Him?
> (Isaiah 59:1-3).

> ### What is the only way to solve our sin problem?
> (John 3:16, Acts 2:38, 1 John 1:7)

1. As far as Jesus is concerned His death at Calvary provided forgiveness for our present, past and all future sins as long as we come to Him, repent and receive that forgiveness. Therefore if we commit sins, let us repent immediately and seek forgiveness from the Lord God according to His Word (1 John 1:9).

2. Mature Christians are extremely sensitive to the least or smallest sin. Search your heart to see if you have harboured any sins that you were negligent in confessing to the Lord. Pray now and seek His forgiveness.

CAIN, THE FIRST MURDERER AND ABEL, THE FIRST MARTYR

1. **Today's Scripture**
   Genesis 4:1-26
2. **Memory Verse**
   Genesis 4:7
   "If you do good I will accept you. But if you do not do good, sin is ready to attack you. Sin wants you. But you must rule over it."
3. **Reference Scripture**
   Exodus 20:13
4. **Objectives**
   a. Let us learn the tragic nature of sin through the crimes of Cain and Lamech. Let us exert our utmost effort to keep ourselves as far away from sin as possible.
   b. Let us learn the reason why Cain's altar of sacrifice was not accepted, and renew our right attitude towards God.
   c. Let us learn the right attitude of worship towards God by studying Abel's altar.

LEADING QUESTIONS

> **What did Cain and Abel offer to God respectively?**
> (Genesis 4:3-4)
> a) _____ b) _____

> **What did Cain answer to the Lord God when he was asked about Abel's whereabouts?**
> (Genesis 4:9)

> **Whom did God give to Adam and Eve in the place of the murdered Abel?**
> (Genesis 4:25-26)

TODAY'S MESSAGE

So far, we have studied Adam and Eve and the curse that was placed on them when they were put out of the garden of Eden as the result of their transgression and fall. After that, Adam and Eve had to toil and sweat with many thorns and thistles to earn their meal. Our merciful Father allowed Adam and Eve to have children according to His blessing so that they could be fruitful and multiply, but Cain, born under Adam's curse, murdered his brother, Abel.

Through the first murderer Cain, and the first murdered person Abel, we will study in this lesson the first appearance of misery in the human race after Adam's transgression and fall.

The First Murderer – Cain

Cain was born as the first son to Adam and Eve. Though Adam and Eve had been made perfect, Cain and Abel were born under the sin of their parents. Therefore, Cain and Abel were brought into this world with the blood of original sin already flowing through them (Romans 5:12-14).

They certainly should have known from their father, Adam, the sad story of mankind's failure and also the prophecy that to redeem fallen man from sin, a woman's child would crush the head of the snake, Satan (Genesis 3:1-21).

They were taught to build an altar before God, kill a lamb and shed its blood for a sacrifice offering as their confession of faith in God's redemptive plan. We see this very plainly by remembering the act of God Who had killed animals to clothe Adam and Eve with the animals' skins.

Time passed. Cain and Abel grew up and when they built their own households, they respectively built their altars before God too.

Cain offered God some food from the ground while Abel offered God the best parts of his best sheep. God sent down fire from heaven and accepted Abel's sacrifice but did not accept Cain's (Leviticus 9:24, Judges 6:21, 1 Kings 18:38).

Seeing that God accepted only Abel's offering, Cain harboured a grudge and hatred against his younger brother Abel, and eventually murdered him in the field. Abel's death became the first death of mankind and also the first murder in human history. Cain became the first murderer and was cast out by God.

Cain's Altar Rejected

Why did God send down fire on Abel's sacrifice but reject Cain's?

The first reason Cain's sacrifice was not accepted was because he came to the Lord God with a disobedient heart.

It turned out that Cain tried to force God to accept his offering in his own way instead of following God's explicit instruction to bring a baby lamb. Cain's disregard for God's Word is just like the religion of humanism today, with the attitude of a man-oriented worship, an overbearing attitude and action which dares to use God merely as a vehicle for man's accomplishment.

The second reason Cain's sacrifice was not accepted was because he denied that he was a sinner. When he came before God, he did not depend upon the blood of a baby lamb. Instead he brought what he thought was good, grown out of the cursed ground. In other words, with a mind filled with human pride, Cain thought that he could boldly stand before God with the fruit of his toil, instead of shedding the blood of a lamb as a token of his faith in God's promise.

The third reason his sacrifice was not accepted was because Cain disregarded God's promise and did not believe in Him who had promised to send the descendant of a woman, the baby "lamb", Jesus Christ, for the redemption of all men. He also did not respect God's command to bring a lamb to sacrifice as a token of his faith in God's promise. His disbelief was manifested through his behaviour in the matter of sacrifice. He turned his face away from God, so God did not send the fire on Cain's offering and did not accept him.

The Altar of the First Martyr, Abel

Why was God so pleased with Abel's sacrifice?

Abel manifested a true faith in God with absolute obedience and trust in Him.

Most of all Abel built the altar according to God's instructions, to please God, not to please his own will. In other words, Abel offered a God-centred sacrifice, not a man- or self-centred sacrifice.

Further, Abel was humble in confessing that he was a sinner and showed obedience and faith by offering a lamb on the altar, believing that God would send the redeemer, Jesus, to shed His blood for the atonement of Abel's sin, as was taught through his father Adam.

And God responded to Abel's offering and accepted him with pleasure.

Before we see what Cain and Abel sacrificed on their altars, however, we should first examine the hearts of these altar builders and see whether their hearts were set to do the will of God or to do their own will. Are our actions taken according to God's will or man's will; through my righteous work or Jesus' blood, disbelief in Jesus or believing in Him as Saviour? We must carefully check our heart attitude and faith because even today the fire of the Holy Spirit of God will be present in our lives dependent upon our heart attitude and faith in God.

Therefore, remembering Jesus' warning, we should always take heed to have the right attitude toward our Heavenly Father.

> *"Not everyone who says that I am his Lord will enter the kingdom of heaven. The only people who will enter the kingdom of heaven are those who do the things that my Father in heaven wants."* (Matthew 7:21)

CLOSING QUESTIONS

> ### What did Jesus say about murdering?
> (Matthew 5:21-22, 1 John 3:15)

> ### What did Abel offer to God and what did Abel hear from God?
> (Hebrews 11:4)

> ### What is the pleasing sacrifice to the Lord God?
> (1 Samuel 15:22, Proverbs 15:8, Isaiah 1: 11-15)

APPLICATION

1. Hatred and anger incite crimes such as murder. If you are now harbouring even a small amount of jealousy or anger against anyone, you should repent and confess your sin to God. Pray and be patient before the Lord.

2. Look into your heart and see what your attitude is when you attend worship services. Always build the altar that pleases God, as Abel did.

THE THREE SONS OF
NOAH

1. **Today's Scripture**
   Genesis 9:1-28
2. **Memory Verse**
   1 Corinthians 10:12
   So anyone who thinks he is standing strong should be careful not to fall.
3. **Reference Scripture**
   Genesis 6:1-22
4. **Objectives**
   a. Let us apprehend the nature of sin that permeates the world widely day by day. Let us try our very best to avoid sin in our living.
   b. Let us remember that faith not only saves one who believes in Jesus, but it can also save his whole household.
   c. Observing the consequence of the deeds of Noah's sons, let us be watchful in our daily living. Let us try not to slacken the due restraint that is essential in our faith life.

LEADING QUESTIONS

> ### What was the situation of human beings in the days of Noah?
> (Genesis 6:5)

> ### How many of Noah's family were saved?
> (Genesis 7:7)

> ### What did Noah do after the judgement of the flood? What kind of shameful behaviour did Noah display then?
> (Genesis 9:20-21)

TODAY'S MESSAGE

After their departure from God, people were getting more and more vile. When Noah came on the scene, the world was full to the brim with iniquity. Seeing all this, God was so grieved that He wanted to destroy man whom He had made and erase him from the earth by flood. But He chose Noah, a righteous man, to build an ark so that those who loved God could be saved. Through the example of the ark of Noah and the judgement of the flood, this lesson will present the state of the sinners who departed from God.

Mankind in Noah's Time

God created mankind so that He would receive glory. Yet far from returning the glory to God, people disobeyed His commands and even rebelled against Him. One man went further against God and even murdered his brother whom God made after His image and likeness. On the earth, descendants of Seth had begun to take the daughters of men as their wives (Genesis 6:1-2).

Even the descendants of pious Seth who had worshipped God too were departing from God. When they left God they too soaked in the dissipation of the world and committed all kinds of sins. The Bible records this state as follows:

> *The Lord saw that the human beings on the earth were very wicked. He also saw that their thoughts were only about evil all the time.* (Genesis 6:5)

Seeing the wickedness of the descendants of Seth, God repented that he had created man and sighed, because it was not the will of God for man to degenerate to debauchery (Genesis 6:6). God sighed over the people of Noah's days because the people did not apprehend their sinful nature nor try to find God. They did not know where they came from, what they were living for or where they were eventually going.

God determined to destroy the wicked world so He asked Noah to warn the people of coming judgement and to build the ark of safety.

Today, God is still warning sinners in the world about His coming judgement and He is inviting them to come into the ark of Jesus Christ. The God we trust is a sin-judging God of righteousness but at the same time He is a God of love who wants to redeem the sinners.

The Ark of Noah and the Flood

Certainly God chose Noah because he was a righteous man, but also, the name "Noah" in Hebrew means "comfort" and "peace". In the middle of the murmur, resentment and rebellion of the people in that day, Noah was full of comfort and peace like the meaning of his name. He was a man of obedience. He was living in faith and he believed what God had said. His faith enabled him not only to overcome but to give comfort and peace during the difficult life in the ark, while he was waiting out the 40 days of flood and the six months after the flood.

So the first lesson we can learn is that when we are facing tests and storms of life like the flood in Noah's time, we too should have the same peace and comfort that Noah had.

Second, God told Noah to build the ark. This ark is symbolic of Christ. As Noah went into the ark, we should go into Jesus Christ and close tightly the door of our hearts so that the temptations and sins all around us cannot enter.

Third, just as Noah looked up at the sky through the window that was opened above, we should look up only to our Heavenly Father through the window of prayer instead of looking down on the storms of our life.

Last, just as the flood of Noah's day caused the wicked people to perish in their sins, we too should come into the safety of Jesus Christ to be cleansed of our wickedness so that we will not perish but receive His power to live victorious lives.

Through the above lessons, we can perceive and learn the meaning of the ark of Noah and the judgement of the flood. We too, like Noah, can live great and successful lives.

The Three Sons of Noah

After they had been given God's covenant that He would never again judge the world by flood to destroy all mankind, the family of Noah began to cultivate land and plant vineyards. One day Noah drank of the wine, became drunk and behaved in a disgraceful manner, sleeping uncovered in broad daylight. Grapes ferment easily and the juice quickly becomes wine. Wine makes one lose self-control, degrades integrity and also motivates others to become tempted and commit sins.

Though Noah was a godly and righteous man, when he became careless he committed a shameful deed. When we are not filled with the Holy Spirit but become neglectful, Satan can plant a seed of sin, even in the minds of believers, which will take root and later grow and branch out into many sins.

By being drunk, Noah caused his second son to commit a sin. Ham saw his father naked and slandered him right away to his brothers.

But Noah's other two sons, Shem and Japheth, covered their father's disgrace and rebuked Ham. Later Noah found out what his sons did and blessed Shem and Japheth but cursed Ham.

First he blessed Shem, *"May the Lord, the God of Shem, be praised!"* (Genesis 9:26). Shem, at Noah's command and blessing, became the leader of religious power. The Oriental people came from Shem and Christianity came through the lineage of Shem.

Second, Japheth was blessed to enjoy a share of Shem's blessing (Genesis 9:27). As a matter of fact Christianity, which originated from the children of Shem, shined its light into the race of Japheth, the white people, so that they were enlarged, grew under the Christian culture and they are still enjoying a blessed life materially.

Last, Ham was cursed and became a servant to his brethren (Genesis 9:25). Throughout history, the children of Ham have lived as servants in many cases. It was not because God made them slaves but it was the punitive results of Ham's sin.

As long as we are living in this world we can never be perfect. Even the believers of Jesus occasionally committed sins as Noah or Ham did; but as long as we are not taking off the helmet of salvation but are being filled with the Holy Spirit, we are able to avoid Noah's failure and we will not only experience his success but will continue to live in the success.

CLOSING QUESTIONS

> ### What spread to all men as the result of sin?
> (Romans 5:12)

> ### By what was Noah able to build the ark in preparation for the flood?
> (Hebrews 11:7)

> ### Why should we control ourselves and be careful?
> (1 Peter 5:8)

Now consider the application of this lesson which you will find on the next page.

APPLICATION

1. Compare the trend in the days of Noah with the trend of today and share with each other what your common findings are.

2. The ark of Noah is symbolic of Jesus Christ. Share with each other the personal experiences of great comfort and peace you received by coming into the ark in Jesus Christ after you had suffered in sin, and glorify the name of the Lord Jesus.

3. The Korean race is also a descendant of the blessed Shem lineage and was called by God as a spiritual priesthood. It is our prayer that God will use us as a spiritual priesthood to reach the world for Jesus and to proclaim the fullness of the Holy Spirit.

THE BUILDERS OF THE
TOWER OF BABEL

1. **Today's Scripture**
   Genesis 11:1-9
2. **Memory Verse**
   Proverbs 12:15
   > *A foolish person thinks he is doing right. But a wise person listens to advice.*
3. **Reference Scripture**
   Matthew 12:25
4. **Objectives**
   a. Let us do our best to make both our private life and church life truly Christ-centred.
   b. Let us be humble before God at all times that we may not fall into the sin of pride.
   c. Let us remember that we will be destroyed if we despise the Word of God. We should always honour the Word of God.

LEADING QUESTIONS

> **How many languages did mankind have originally?**
> (Genesis 11:1)

> **Where did the people build the Tower of Babel?**
> (Genesis 11:2)

> **What was their purpose in building the tower?**
> (Genesis 11:3-4)

TODAY'S MESSAGE

People have always, and still are, endeavouring to magnify themselves and lift up their hearts to succeed in life without God. Adam and Eve fell in the attempt to be like God and now the descendants of Noah also defied God, planning to reach heaven through building the Tower of Babel. They built a city and a tower so they would never be scattered again. It was also to be their safe place in case a flood would come again in the future, but above all, their desire was to display their own power and glory through it, but they failed to complete it.

This lesson will cover how man failed to build the tower, because his motives and attitudes towards God were wrong.

A Babel Tower of Confusion

The number one factor in their failure to complete the tower was the confusion which came upon them. "Babel" means confusion. When they were busily constructing the tower, God confounded their language. Immediately they thought differently, talked differently and acted differently. All of a sudden the builders realized they were incapable of cooperating together to build the tower and they were divided into groups that spoke the same language.

Of course, our Heavenly Father is pleased when we are united with one accord for the sake of His glory and good will. The builders of the Babel Tower were also united; however, they were going against God so He had to stop their building by confounding their language.

Even today, to achieve a certain thing successfully there must be unity. To lead a successful life we should always work in unity and watch that no confusion approaches our living. Jesus Christ said:
> *"Every kingdom that is fighting against itself will be destroyed. And every city that is divided will fall. And every family that is divided cannot succeed."* (Matthew 12:25)

When we are divided, we fall. The devil always causes confusion to divide people so that God's work will be thwarted and people will fall away. Therefore, we must be on guard that the enemy of our soul will not bring division. We must remove any kind of confusion and disharmony in our hearts, homes, society, churches and homecell groups. We should do our utmost to allow the Holy Spirit to keep us in the unity of the Spirit so that we become one in Jesus.

A Babel Tower of Pride

Another reason for the descendants of Noah failing to complete the tower was that they were filled with pride before God and attempted to place themselves higher than God. Pride is against God's will and our sin always originates in pride. Proverbs 16:18 teaches:
> *Pride will destroy a person. A proud attitude leads to ruin.*

From the very beginning their motive in proposing the tower contradicted God's will.

If they wanted to build the tower in that location for the purpose of having a close-knit unity among themselves, that was a direct challenge to the command of God because after the flood God commanded them to have many young ones and grow in number upon the earth (Genesis 8:17).

If they wanted to build the tower in preparation for a future flood, that was a sin of disbelief of the promise of God:

"Floodwaters will never again destroy all life on the earth." (Genesis 9:15)

If they wanted to display their power and honour to the coming generation through the tower, that is clearly an act of pride placing themselves ahead of God and His glory. They deserved ill for their deed and for this reason all of their purposes were not achieved, but failed.

Therefore, we should always guard against pride. When we become conceited and boast of every small success, the sure thing that follows is destruction. Pride always brings along a "Tower of Babel" and the "Babel" always causes confusion. We must always be humble believers before God and other people.

A Babel Tower of Rebellion

Most of all, the builders of the Babel Tower suffered confusion, chaos and failure because they esteemed God's Word too lightly.

God had commanded the children of Noah to multiply and spread over all the earth, but they told each other in Genesis 11:4:

"Let's build for ourselves a city and a tower. And let's make the top of the tower reach high into the sky. We will become famous. If we do this, we will not be scattered over all the earth."

This was a direct challenge and rebellion against the command of God.

When they rebelled against God, God caused chaos by confounding their language, a wise move on God's part. When the people were not able to communicate with each other, they could not understand each other, and where there is no understanding, there is jealousy, resentment, strife and faction.

Today, if the sin of despising God's Word enters any individual, home, society or nation, confusion begins, smoulders, and eventually it destroys the foundation and existence of the person or society. The "tower" that is called the "life" of an individual, the "tower" that is called the "home" of a family and the "tower" called "society" or a "nation", collapse though the sin of opposing the command of the Lord God. Human history sufficiently proves this. We all know only too well those countries and churches which feared God's Word, became powerful and prospered, while those countries that despised God and the gospel are impoverished today and are still failing.

For us to lead a successful life, we must eliminate all the elements of confusion and division that may be called the "Towers of Babel" in our lives. Let us eradicate all the Babelic poisons in our everyday living and march forward in the complete harmony of the Holy Spirit. When we do so, all our purposes and our work will succeed in bearing fruit and we shall enjoy God's abundant blessings.

CLOSING QUESTIONS

> ### According to 1 Corinthians 14:33, what do you think of our God?

> ### What will happen eventually to the person who despises the Word of God?
> (Proverbs 13:13)

> ### How should our thoughts, mind, and love be?
> (Philippians 2:2)

APPLICATION

1. Let us discuss what the "Babel Towers" could be in our everyday living.

2. Let us search our hearts to find out whether we are building a Tower of Babel. If we are proud before God and we are faced with confusion and disharmony in our lives, how can we solve this?

SODOM AND GOMORRAH

1. **Today's Scripture**
   Genesis 19:12-28
2. **Memory Verse**
   Genesis 19:24-25
   > *The Lord sent a rain of burning sulphur down from the sky on Sodom and Gomorrah. So the Lord destroyed those cities. He also destroyed the whole Jordan Valley, everyone living in the cities and even all the plants.*
3. **Reference Scripture**
   Genesis 18:16-33
   Isaiah 1:9-10
4. **Objectives**
   a. Through the scene of destruction of Sodom and Gomorrah, let us learn that God is righteous and He hates sin.
   b. By knowing the fact that all the wicked will be destroyed, let us strive to lead a pure life that is far from sin.
   c. Let us have a pure faith by always repenting immediately if we do sin.

LEADING QUESTIONS

> **With what did God destroy Sodom and Gomorrah?**
> (Genesis 19:24)

> **What did Lot's wife become when she looked back?**
> (Genesis 19:26)
> **What is the spiritual lesson for us?**

> **To what can we attribute Lot's salvation from the judgement of Sodom?**
> (Genesis 19:29)

TODAY'S MESSAGE

The picture of Sodom and Gomorrah and its destruction is one of the most degrading views of man when he departs from God. In this lesson, through the tragedy of Sodom and Gomorrah, we will examine the plain fact that the ultimate fate of the wicked is ruin and judgement. We will also learn how we should deal with sin.

The Ruin of Unbelieving People

Abraham was the father of faith. He always looked up to God, and grew in His grace and love. As he matured in faith, he was able to live a victorious life. However, there were also men who perished because they lived without faith.

They were the people of Sodom and Gomorrah who were exceedingly wicked sinners before the Lord (Genesis 13:13). They had become so debased that they even demanded for their sodomy two angels sent by God. At last, with the one exception of Lot's family, they were judged by God's wrath and everyone perished. Today, all men are sinners before God. Moreover, the sin of despising and jesting about God's word of warning is a most serious sin.

Lot's sons-in-law took the warning of their father-in-law, Lot, as a joke when they were told to hurry and get out of the city because the Lord would destroy the city (Genesis 19:14). As a result they too perished, together with all the people of Sodom. Their wrong attitude of taking God's Word as a joke because they did not have faith. There are some people who make their opportunity for salvation an occasion of destruction.

Now, look at Lot's wife, a woman of less faith. The angels saved her life, even seizing her by the hand. Yet, ignoring the word of warning not to look back, she committed the sin of disobedience, looked back at Sodom and became a pillar of salt. She did the same thing her sons-in-law did – she did not listen to the Word of God. She looked back because her love for the things she was leaving behind in Sodom was greater than her desire to be saved. So she perished.

Finally, we now look at the shameful behaviour of Lot's two daughters. The two daughters were saved because two angels took them by the hand and led them out of the city yet, absurd as it was, after their salvation they drank in a cave, slept with their father and produced children of sin: the father of the Moabites and the father of the Ammonites. So Lot's family, who loved the world and compromised with the sins of the world, lived in misery.

The Wicked Shall Perish

Psalm 37:9 says:
> *Evil people will be sent away. But people who trust the Lord will inherit the land.*

Wickedness cannot last long because it will be judged not by man but by God, Who is righteous and eternal.

Even today, there are many cities like Sodom and Gomorrah all around us, filled with the same kind of people living in utter wickedness. There is one type of "Sodom and Gomorrah" that despises the warning of the gospel without acknowledging sin. There is another "Sodom and Gomorrah" that is called communism, rebelling against God and trampling down human dignity and freedom.

In this end time, the world is getting more and more wicked, so we should pray to our Heavenly Father more fervently that those sinners may come quickly into the grace of God.

The days of the wicked are not long. Throughout history, we have seen numerous Sodoms and Gomorrahs that have not lasted long but were soon judged and punished. Whether it is an individual, a society or a nation, those who do not repent of their sins are doomed to be judged and will perish.

On the contrary, the Word of God promised:
> People who are not proud will inherit the land. They will enjoy complete peace. (Psalm 37:11)

God always takes the side of the meek. He speaks for them and helps them to be led to His kingdom. Therefore, as we trust in God we can achieve great things, inheriting the land, destroying the wickedness, but bringing along love, righteousness and freedom in our lives.

The Correct Attitude Towards Sin

The incident of Sodom and Gomorrah shows symbolically that all people in the world are sinners and the end of those sinners is the judgement of death.

We too, like the people of Sodom and Gomorrah, were sinners in this world, but God sent Jesus to proclaim the gospel and to deliver us by His hand from the judgement of destruction. We obeyed God so we were delivered from the terrible consequences that would have led us to a terrible Sodom. Therefore, we believers in Jesus Christ are no longer under the judgement of damnation.

As long as we are living on this earth, however, we are not totally immune from the temptation of sin. Often, like Lot, even after we have been saved, we are tempted by sin and fall. In such cases we believers will generally react in one of the following ways.

First, there is the humiliating attitude of making many excuses after one has sinned. If we are long-winded, we will attempt to enumerate our many many excuses to both God and our conscience, and God will loathe our self-righteous attitude instead of showering us with His sympathy, mercy and forgiveness.

Another attitude when confronted directly with sin is an attitude of struggling to fight with our own human resolution and power. If we fight alone against the sins and we make resolutions never to sin again, we will always be beaten, much less win over the sin.

Finally, there is a correct attitude towards sin. When we have tried hard to resist but have succumbed to temptation and have sinned, the best thing to do is to confess honestly to God that we are helpless to win over sin by our own might. Then we should pray and ask for God's forgiveness and help through the power of the Holy Spirit. When we sin, we should always confess immediately and seek His forgiveness. Only then will cleansing come with forgiveness and peace.

Today, let us confess to the Lord Jesus that we are powerless over sin and pray that the law of the Spirit of life in Christ Jesus, which sets us free from the law of sin and death, will truly keep us free! When we pray like this, the Holy Spirit will help us. He will strengthen our willpower and lead us to win over every temptation of sin one by one, so that we continue to enjoy victorious Christian living.

CLOSING QUESTIONS

> ### How many righteous people were needed after all to save Sodom and Gomorrah?
> (Genesis 18:32-33)

> ### What does the Bible call the rulers and people who do not listen to the Word of God?
> (Isaiah 1:9-10)

> ### What must we do after we have sinned?
> (1 John 1:9)

Now consider the application of this lesson which you will find on the next page.

APPLICATION

1. These days, the flood of sin is rising higher in the world than in the days of Sodom and Gomorrah. Let us always pray and be watchful that the influence of this evil trend does not invade our hearts and develop into action.

2. Let us discuss together other cases in the Bible where people were judged by death because of their sin.

THE POISONOUS SNAKES AND THE BRONZE SNAKE

1. **Today's Scripture**
   Numbers 21:4-9
2. **Memory Verse**
   John 3:14-15
   > *"Moses lifted up the snake in the desert. It is the same with the Son of Man. The Son of Man must be lifted up too. Then everyone who believes in him can have eternal life."*
3. **Reference Scripture**
   John 3:1-15
4. **Objectives**
   a. Through the judgement of the poisonous snakes upon Israel, let us remember that grumbling against God is a serious sin.
   b. Let us understand that the only way of deliverance from God's judgement for our sin is Jesus Christ.
   c. As the people of Israel looked up to the bronze snake and lived, let us look up to Jesus Christ every day and live!

LEADING QUESTIONS

> **When Israel grumbled against God and Moses, what was it about?**
> (Numbers 21:5)

> **What did these Israelites do after God sent poisonous snakes?**
> (Numbers 21:7)

> **What happened to those who looked upon the bronze snake?**
> (Numbers 21:9)

TODAY'S MESSAGE

The condition of man after his departure from God is always misery. On their journey towards the land of Canaan after their deliverance from Egypt, the Israelites committed many sins, stumbling into the temptations of Satan and falling many times. As a result, they were judged by God. As we study God's judgement of sending poisonous snakes upon them when they sinned, we will learn the result of their sin of grumbling and the way of God's salvation for them.

Judgement by the Poisonous Snakes

The people of Israel had to travel through the wilderness to reach the promised land of Canaan that God gave. While crossing the wilderness, they lost heart and became extremely discouraged. The road was rough. There was not sufficient food, nor water, and their legs were very tired. They were dissatisfied with everything and they began to grumble and complain against God and Moses.

When the grumbling voice of the Israelites rose high, from somewhere unknown poisonous snakes came and bit those people. Many died in agony and pain. Realizing they had sinned, they repented of their grumbling against God and asked Moses to pray for their salvation from the snakes.

> The people came to Moses and said, "We sinned when we grumbled at you and the Lord. Pray that the Lord will take away these snakes."

Seeing the people of Israel repent, Moses prayed to God and God commanded:

> "Make a bronze snake and put it on a pole. If anyone is bitten, he should look at it. Then he will live."

Moses obeyed and made a bronze snake. He set the snake on a pole and asked the people who were bitten to look upon the bronze snake. Amazingly, as they looked, they recovered and lived.

Jesus Christ, our Bronze Snake

The story of the people of Israel who rebelled and grumbled against God is a picture of all of us sinners in the world. And the poisonous snakes symbolize sin or Satan. The Israelites died in pain after having been bitten by the snakes, and this shows that we will be judged by death for our sins if we don't repent.

Our healing and deliverance from the poison of sin comes only by looking to Jesus Christ on the cross in faith, just as Israel lived by looking up to the bronze snake in faith in the wilderness.

Why did God send the poisonous snakes to the Israelites?

First, to awaken them to realize they had sinned against God by grumbling against Him and Moses. Grumbling and resentment are sins that grieve the heart of God and cause His anger. The tougher our situation becomes, the more we should thank God instead of grumbling and complaining before Him. We don't know how God is leading but we should always know He has our best interests in mind and soon all things will work together to bring us to His promised land or to the answer to our prayer. Thanksgiving is the song of God. Grumbling and resentment are the songs of the devil.

Second, God sent poisonous snakes to the people of Israel so that they would confess, repent and be forgiven by Him. After they received the judgement of poisonous snakes they became aware of their sins. They also became aware of the fact that their lives could not be saved by their own might. That caused them to seek God's forgiveness and salvation and God sent the bronze snake to redeem them. Even today, our times of trouble and problems in life can become a turning point for us to look up to Jesus, just as the Israelites obeyed and looked up at the bronze snake on the pole. God's purpose in all of our sufferings is to bring us to a place where we break our stubbornness before Him and repent. Then, we too will see Jesus.

Third, the purpose of sending poisonous snakes was to bring death to the ones who did not repent of their sins and did not even bother to look up to the bronze snake. Those who grumbled in a moment of anger, but immediately repented after having been bitten by poisonous snakes, all recovered by looking up at the bronze snake on the pole. But those who did not, died without exception. It is the same today. For those who resist till the end and refuse to repent and receive the gospel of Jesus, even though God breaks them and they suffer many hardships and pain, who resist the urging to open the door of their hearts, there is no other outcome than to receive the judgement of eternal damnation and be lost.

Behold the Bronze Snake!

The bronze snake on the high pole was a foreshadow of the coming Jesus Who would hang on the cross for our sins (John 3:14-15). As the bronze snake was hung on a wooden pole and all those who looked up in faith were healed, so today as we look up to Jesus Christ, we will find salvation and deliverance for every sin and problem we will ever have.

First, to be born again we need to see Jesus Christ nailed on the cross, taking our place. We were all bitten by the snake of sin, so in our bloodstream the same poison which flowed in Adam is flowing in us. To live without this sin, we must look to Jesus Christ Who hung high on the cross.

Second, to be cleansed daily from our sins we must still look up to

Jesus Christ Who hung on the cross. During our lifetime, we are bitten many times by the snake of sin, but the precious blood of Jesus always cleanses and heals us when we ask for forgiveness.

Third, to experience God's love daily, we should always continue to look to Jesus Christ. Who understands us and still loves us with an unfailing love like Jesus? When we are utterly lonely and weary in life, we sometimes try to receive consolation from friends or family, but instead of receiving consolation we often receive more hurt or they put salt on our open wounds and our emptiness remains with no comfort. But Jesus loves us with an unchanging love and when we look to Him, we will receive His great love and comfort that always heals.

Last, Jesus Christ's death and resurrection is our title deed of salvation. He signed the "deed" for our salvation with His precious blood. When fear, uncertainty, doubts or scepticism of life creeps into our hearts, we must again look up to Jesus on the cross. When we behold Him, the healing power of the Holy Spirit will work within us confirming our salvation and also pouring in new hope and joy of life.

CLOSING QUESTIONS

Why were some of the people of Israel destroyed?
(1 Corinthians 10:9)

What must we do when we have sinned?
(Psalm 78:34, 1 John 1:9)

When we are sorrowful and we see Jesus, what will He give to us?
(John 16:22)

Now consider the application of this lesson which you will find on the next page.

APPLICATION

1. Share with each other some of the specific cases in your daily living when we must behold Jesus Christ on the cross.

2. All people are sinners, bitten by the snake of sin, and all believers of Jesus Christ are beholders of the bronze snake on the pole, who repented before God and obeyed God's Word. Let us pray that the healing power of Jesus Christ will come upon our family members and friends.

THE DISOBEDIENT
KING SAUL

1. **Today's Scripture**
   1 Samuel 15:1-35
2. **Memory Verse**
   1 Samuel 15:22
   > *But Samuel answered, "What pleases the Lord more: burnt offerings and sacrifices or obedience? It is better to obey God than to offer a sacrifice. It is better to listen to God than to offer the fat of male sheep."*
3. **Reference Scripture**
   Deuteronomy 30:9-10
4. **Objectives**
   a. Seeing the tragic end of disobedient Saul, let us always be careful to obey God's Word.
   b. Let us know what God really wants of us. He wants our humble obedience to the leading of the Holy Spirit.
   c. Let us all become faithful workers and the precious vessels that God can use.

LEADING QUESTIONS

> ### What did Saul do about the command of God that was given to him through Samuel?
> (1 Samuel 15:8-9)

> ### What did God say after He saw Saul's action?
> (1 Samuel 15:10-11)

> ### What was the primary reason for God rejecting Saul as king?
> (1 Samuel 15:26)

TODAY'S MESSAGE

God sternly judges even His chosen vessels when they challenge His authority. That is because God is a God of righteousness and justice as much as he is a God of love. Though Saul was chosen to be the first king of the united Israel, he ended in misery and was removed from his throne because he disobeyed God. Through the failure of King Saul, we will learn what our God indeed wants of us and also the characteristics of the kind of man He uses.

The Reprobate King who was Rejected by God

Through the prophet Samuel, Saul received God's commandment to attack wicked Amalek. The Amalekites were idol worshippers and adversaries of God. Because of God's plan to preserve Israel and also to receive glory though them, God commanded Saul:

"Now go, attack the Amalekites. Destroy everything that belongs to them as an offering to the Lord. Don't let anything live. Put to death men and women, children and small babies. Kill the cattle and sheep, camels and donkeys."

King Saul organised the forces and by the power of God he defeated the Amalekites. However, in an attempt to receive some glory through the victory of this war, Saul did not obey all of God's commandments. Instead, He spared the king of the Amalekites alive, the best of the sheep, cattle, calves, lambs and all that was good and took them home. He did not obey God's command to destroy all the people and animals of the Amalekites.

In anger, the Lord God rebuked Saul through Samuel for his disobedience and declared that there is no sacrifice and worship that can be substituted for simply obeying God. Even so, Saul was concerned first with his being disgraced before the people of Israel, instead of returning at once to repent sincerely before God.

Eventually, King Saul was rejected by God, lost his throne, lost the presence of God and as a result he died miserably during a war with the Philistines (1 Samuel 31:4).

What does our Heavenly Father Want of Us?

If we compare the lives of Saul and David we can see very well that God wants obedience and repentance from us. Both of them were kings chosen by God and they both committed many sins. But, strangely enough, God rejected Saul but forgave and restored David, though he committed serious sins.

What was the reason? There was a clear reason. David was completely broken and contrite when he sinned. Though he was king of the country, when he transgressed, he humbly acknowledged what he did and repented immediately when his sin was pointed out by the prophet. He did not excuse himself when he was reprimanded for his transgressions. David was quick to repent and cry out for mercy and forgiveness but Saul became bitter and went away from God. When God sees a repentant heart, He is always full of mercy to forgive and restore. As God saw the humble heart of David, He not only forgave him but also restored him.

But Saul was different. He wilfully disobeyed God's instructions. In addition, when his sin was pointed out and he was reprimanded by God, instead of repenting, he tried to justify and rationalize what he had done. Furthermore, when he was told by Samuel that the Lord had rejected him from being king over Israel, Saul still begged and pleaded to remain as king instead of acknowledging his sin and repenting. God saw Saul's heart was not in returning to him.

There is not one single person living in this world who has not sinned. During our lives all of us, without exception, commit many sins, stumble and fall. But one thing we should never do before God is to rationalize what we have done and justify our actions.

When God knocks at the door of our heart by His Word, the only thing we can do is to break before the presence of our holy and righteous God and repent of our sins. When we do so, God will not only forgive us but will also restore us in His mercy and love so that we are able to stand before Him forgiven, without losing time.

Therefore, when you sin, do not delay earnestly repenting and seeking forgiveness from God. Our good God who forgave King David will also forgive you and He will restore to you His abundant blessings.

The Vessels that God Uses

Truly, all of us in the world are living in pursuit of our own profit. But those who have been chosen and called through Jesus Christ live to manifest the glory of God. In that context, all believers of Jesus Christ are chosen vessels of God.

What must we do to become a good vessel that God can use?
First, to become a God-chosen vessel, we must be cleansed by the precious blood of Jesus, present our lives to God, and dedicate ourselves completely. We must kneel at His feet and empty ourselves to become a fully committed vessel to serve our Lord. This should be our confession: "O Father, take me. Perform Your will through me and glorify Your name through me wherever I am."

Second, to become a vessel used by God, we must have a vision and dreams according to His Word. Though we have no visible proof to our eyes, no audible sound to our ears, and we have no tangible proof in our hands to confirm He is fulfilling His plan through us, and though we may sometimes despair, we must steadfastly hold on to the belief that God can do all things. When we have this much confidence in the Lord we shall become precious vessels that God can use.

Third, to become a vessel used by God, we must give thanksgiving to Him under any circumstance. No matter how severely your situation oppresses you, take God's Word as your answer with thanksgiving, and with impregnable faith just obey Him. Through your faith, the Spirit of God will conquer and control your situation and the name of our Heavenly Father will be glorified. When the will of God is done through us like this, we will become precious vessels that God uses.

CLOSING QUESTIONS

What blessing follows those who obey God and keep His laws?
(Deuteronomy 30:9-10)

What will happen if we do not turn away from our sin?
(Psalm 7:12)

How did the Apostle Paul compare God to a potter making jars, or vessels?
(Romans 9:21-24, EB & AV)

Now consider the application of this lesson which you will find on the next page.

APPLICATION

1. Saul started wonderfully as a king but ended in failure. Let us look back on our faith life and share with each other how the beginning of our Christian life and our present life are different. Our successful spiritual growth comes when we are obedient to God but our failure comes when we disobey God.

2. What God wants of us is obedience and repentance. Let us share specific examples of how we can really obey God's Word in our daily living.

GOD-GRIEVING
SINS

1. **Today's Scripture**
   1 Corinthians 10:1-13
2. **Memory Verse**
   1 Corinthians 10:12-13
   So anyone who thinks he is standing strong should be careful not to fall. The only temptations that you have are the temptations that all people have. But you can trust God. He will not let you be tempted more than you can stand. But when you are tempted, God will also give you a way to escape that temptation. Then you will be able to stand it.
3. **Reference Scripture**
   1 Corinthians 5:7-8
4. **Objectives**
   a. Let us understand clearly the sins that grieve God and let us live as far away from them as possible.
   b. To overcome the temptations of sin and to bring ourselves near to God, let us always be diligent in prayer and the study of His Word.

LEADING QUESTIONS

> ### Who is the spiritual rock that gives life-giving water to us?
> (John 4:14, 1 Corinthians 10:4)

> ### Why were most of the Israelites destroyed in the wilderness?
> (1 Corinthians 10: 5-6)

> ### Why does the Bible record their sin and ruin?
> (1 Corinthians 10:11)

TODAY'S MESSAGE

Through some of the characters of the Old Testament and their experiences, we have so far reviewed several tragic consequences of man's original sin and subsequent sins after his departure from God. God hates sin. He grieves especially when His children commit sin.

In this lesson, by going through some of the representative sins, we will study where man stands now since his fall, in terms of his relationship to God.

The Sin of Idolatry

The number one sin that grieves God the most is the sin of idolatry. In Genesis chapter 32, the people of Israel made a golden calf as their idol and they ate, drank, revelled and committed immoral acts before the idol. People who have made and worshipped idols will receive God's judgement of eternal punishment.

Humanism is an idol for infidels who claim there is no God. They put too much trust in their human intelligence and their own ability, but their final destiny too, can only be the judgement of damnation.

It is possible for even the children of God, believers, to have idols. To us believers, the sin of covetousness is idolatry. If we have something we love more than we love God, it originates from our covetousness and that is idolatry to God. Here, we are not saying only material things are our idols. In some cases it may be a husband, wife, or even children. In other cases, it may be our love of fame or honour in society. But God's wrath is stirred when He sees idolatry. He has already revealed to us clearly through the first and second commandments that we should not worship idols.

Those who worship idols are those who have allowed their altar of worship to crumble. Do you have anything that you love more than you love God? You should not delay any longer but return to God and begin to repair your altar so that you worship only Him. This is only possible for you through the fullness of the Holy Spirit.

The Sin of Adultery and Sexual Immorality

These sins also grieve God heavily. More than 24,000 people of Israel were killed under judgement in one day when they sinned sexually with Moabite women while Israel was camped at Acacia. (Numbers 25:9)

The Bible teaches that God's children who commit adultery will receive God's fierce and unrelenting judgement (1 Corinthians 10:8).

The believer's body is purchased by the blood of Jesus so that he becomes the temple of the Holy Spirit. The Holy Spirit of God dwells in us so we become children of God and members of the body of Jesus

Christ. The Word of God teaches us all other sins are outside our body but sexual sin is a sin against our own body. Therefore committing this sin means despising the Holy Spirit of God who dwells in us, defying His holiness and defiling His Holy Temple, thereby ruining the person's soul.

Sexual sin not only brings separation to the spiritual relationship with God but also it destroys the life of a person. His self-esteem and conscience are marred and his own body becomes diseased. Not only that, sexual sin does great harm to the family and society he belongs to. The cause of the majority of today's marriage breakups is attributed to the immoral acts of husbands and wives outside the marriage relationship.

The Word of God foretold that sexual sin, as a foreboding of the end time, will be sweeping the earth, and today's corrupt sex practices prove the fact openly. The trend of today is to become defiled with those sins so we should be cautious at all times and keep far away from sexual sin and adultery.

The Sin of Putting the Lord to the Test

Another sin we should avoid is putting the Lord God to the test. The people of Israel put the Lord to the test about their food. They contended with God. They complained that He delivered them from Egypt only to have them all starve to death in the desert. God sent down manna and quails for them to eat, but still punished those who tested Him. Nevertheless, the Israelites continually tested God and were judged, bitten by poisonous snakes or attacked by plagues in the wilderness and died.

The same applies today. If we come to God without believing in Him totally, but simply to get healed or to receive peace and make a mental assent that He is the Saviour, or to get God's material blessings, that is putting God to the test. People with that kind of attitude do not worship God as they should. They are only trying to use Him as a means of gratifying their own interests and needs.

God told us He will not be pleased if we turn back. True faith is to trust God in the times of temptation and still praise Him in the darkness of our situation without yielding to sin. Therefore, in times of trouble we should praise our Heavenly Father even more, give Him all the thanks for the work He is doing in our lives and never put Him to the test.

The Sin of Resentment and Grumbling

Resentment and grumbling saddens God. We cannot grow spiritually by harbouring resentment. If a husband resents his wife and the wife resents her husband, love between them will soon fade away. If children resent their parents, the relationship will become strained and the care and love from the parents will get cold. Resentment breaks unity between spouses, creates a sense of distance between parents and children and causes a split in friendships.

Because the children of Israel grumbled against God, God made them wander about in the wilderness. All men over twenty years old, except Joshua and Caleb, died in the wilderness and they could not reach the promised land of milk and honey. Moses' sister, Miriam, was also judged by leprosy for speaking against Moses (Numbers 12:10).

The sin of grumbling takes away the blessings of milk and honey which we received from the Lord, and then it drives us into a desert or wilderness experience where we lose the sense of God's presence. When the troubles of life and horrible situations swoop down upon us, we should still give thanks to the Lord for His goodness instead of resenting or complaining about the situation. Of course this is not easy at all. But when we praise our Heavenly Father and give thanks to Him even in the dark experiences of life, we will see His mighty demonstration of miracles, more than we ever expected.

God's Word is not a set of laws or a heavy yoke. God's Word is our daily food and our resource for victorious living. Therefore, if we are committing the sins of idolatry, sexual immorality or grumbling against God, we should allow God's Word to become a mirror to reflect our true state and repent now.

Let us build anew a pure and holy altar of worship that our Heavenly Father will be pleased with.

CLOSING QUESTIONS

What will become of all idol-makers? (Isaiah 45:16)

Who will not possess God's kingdom? (1 Corinthians 6:9-10)

> **Which sin is a sin against your own body?**
> (1 Corinthians 6:18)

> **Who will take part in the second death which
> is the lake of burning sulphur?**
> (Revelation 21:8)

1. Have you ever put God to the test simply to satisfy your needs? Then repent now and seek His forgiveness.

2. For discussion: Are we really living for the glory of the Lord? Let us always acknowledge the Holy Spirit and lean on Him so that He will direct our paths.

THE CONSEQUENCES OF MAN'S FALL

1. **Today's Scripture**
   Psalm 51:5
   Romans 5:12
2. **Memory Verse**
   Psalm 51:5
   I was brought into this world in sin. In sin my mother gave birth to me.
3. **Reference Scripture**
   2 Kings 21:1-29
   Matthew 5:27-30
   James 4:1-10
4. **Objectives**
   a. Let us understand how disastrous and far-reaching the consequences of man's fall are.
   b. Let us look at the various aspects of the fall and see where we stand by looking at ourselves in the mirror of God's Word.

LEADING QUESTIONS

> ### How does the Psalmist describe himself?
> (Psalm 51:5)

> ### What does God's Word say about the state of all fallen mankind?
> (Romans 3:10)

> ### How does God treat the humble and the proud respectively?
> (James 4:6)

TODAY'S MESSAGE

The account of man's fall in Genesis contains many deep lessons to ponder. From the beginning, man was made with a free will to obey God or not to obey God. But man misused his free will. Because man wanted to be like God, he was seized by arrogance, then he rebelled against God and fell. Because of his sin, his relationship with God was severed. What were the consequences that followed man's fall and what does he look like today?

Covetousness – The First Aspect of Fallen Man

"Covetousness" means "being unsatisfied with what one owns, a wrongful desire to acquire possession of something that does not rightfully belong to the covetous person". This wrongful longing for something that is rightfully another's is the sin most generally committed by fallen mankind.

The sin of covetousness started from the garden of Eden as in Genesis 3:6:

> *The woman saw that the tree was beautiful. She saw that its fruit was good to eat and that it would make her wise. So she took some of its fruit and ate it. She also gave some of the fruit to her husband, and he ate it.*

Here, through the fall of Adam and Eve, at least three aspects of covetousness are shown to us:

1. Covetousness to please man's appetite – "good for food"
2. Covetousness to please man's sight – "pleasant to the eyes"
3. Covetousness to please man's intelligence – "to be desired to make one wise"

But most of all, their hearts were filled with a desire to become like God in a wrong sense and that was the greatest sin of covetousness.

Once this covetousness entered the garden of Eden, such a beautiful garden turned immediately into a ground cursed with thistles and thorns and a forest of judgement for mankind. The Bible explains so vividly what the sin of covetousness brought upon the history of the human race.

At the end of the parable of the foolish wealthy man, God said:

> *"Foolish man! Tonight you will die. So who will get those things you have prepared for yourself?"*

Jesus went on:

> *"This is how it will be for anyone who stores things up only for himself and is not rich toward God."* (Luke 12:20-21)

Jesus teaches us no matter how great a greedy man's treasures may be, if God calls him out, those treasures will become nothing to him.

Covetousness is a sin that makes a person desire more things than he rightfully needs. If he is seized by covetousness to acquire his desires, he deceives, slanders, steals and even commits murder. The Apostle Paul warned:

The love of money causes all kinds of evil. Some people have left the true faith because they want to get more and more money. But they have caused themselves much sorrow. (1 Timothy 6:10)

So put all evil things out of your life: sexual sinning, doing evil, letting evil thoughts control you, wanting things that are evil, and always selfishly wanting more and more. This really means living to serve a false God. (Colossians 3:5)

The sin of covetousness is not committed by individuals only. It is also committed by nations. Century after century, wars break out continually among nations because of their covetousness. Because of covetousness, many employers also illegally take shares of payment that rightfully belong to their workers. This iniquity that is called covetousness has brought all wars, poverty, curses and miserable deaths to mankind.

Pride – The Second Aspect of Fallen Man

Though there are countless kinds of sins, the largest and most common sin is the sin of pride. This sin is manifested in many patterns. Now, we shall initially examine the three major dimensions of pride.

First, there is "spiritual pride", which is the beginning of all sin and also the origin of man's fall. Spiritual pride holds first place among all kinds of pride. Because it is a love for one's own self instead of a love for God, and also it is putting more trust in one's self than in God, this spiritual pride is tantamount to the sin of idolatry. That is why God hates man's spiritual pride so much! Jesus Christ hates the spiritual pride of man also. Our Lord Jesus did not rebuke the awful sinners, the adulterous woman, the tax collectors or prostitutes, but He furiously rebuked the Pharisees who thought they were the most pious believers of God and always boasted in their religion.

Second, there is the pride of knowledge which means the arrogant attitude of the learned toward the less learned and the oppressed. God gave all of us emotional and mental abilities. Yet when we do not think of these powers as gifts from God, a pride of knowledge begins to sprout. The Apostle Paul confirms this in 1 Corinthians 8:1-2:

Knowledge puffs you up with pride, but love builds up. Whoever thinks he knows something does not yet know anything as he should.

We should always try hard to maintain a humble spirit, not thinking more highly of ourselves than we ought (Romans 12:16). Also, we should not forget at any time that reverence for the Lord is the beginning of all our knowledge (Proverbs 1:7).

Third, there is a pride of wealth and authority. The Bible tells us clearly that the power to get wealth and authority comes from the Lord God (Deuteronomy 8:18, 1 Chronicles 29:12, Romans 13:1).

It is ridiculous if we play high-handedly with these God-given gifts as if the wealth and authority belong to us.

Pride must be cleansed away and we must pray to remain humble.

Sexual Sin – The Third Aspect of Fallen Man

In Matthew 12:39 Jesus rebuked the world as *"evil and sinful"*. Today's world is filled with sexual sin and promiscuity just as it was in the days of Sodom and Gomorrah. Sexual sin is the number one consequence of the fall of man. Whether it is a nation, a race or an individual, its decay begins with a spiritual fall, then a mental fall, and then a physical fall. This physical fall means a fall into sexual immorality. By the degree of moral corruption and decay of an individual, society, or nation one can measure the present status of those individuals, societies or nations.

Sexual sin is the easiest of all sins to commit and it is also the sin that brings the most disastrous results. King David could not keep his eyes off temptation, so he finally took Uriah's wife Bathsheba, and committed adultery. Because of his sin, not only King David himself but all of the people of Israel received God's wrath and punishment (1 Samuel chapters 11 and 12).

The sins of adultery and sexual immorality still bring disastrous results. The majority of today's marriage breakups is caused by them. As Satan's sharpest weapons, these sins ruthlessly impair a person's mental health and integrity, and too many times they dampen the futures of young people who had bright hopes and dreams. King Solomon professed:
> *A man who takes part in adultery doesn't have any sense. He will destroy himself. He will be beaten up and disgraced. And his shame will never go away.* (Proverbs 6:32-33)

The finality of fallen mankind is miserable. There seems no way out to salvation. But the Word of God declares:
> *The law came to make people have more sin. But when people had more sin, God gave them more of his grace.* (Romans 5:20)

We received a hope for salvation in the redeeming grace of Jesus Christ, Who delivers us from this disastrous fallen status, and this keeps us day by day – one day at a time.

In other words, without Jesus Christ there is absolutely no way out for us to receive salvation and escape from this fallen status.

CLOSING QUESTIONS

> ### What is the meaning of "free will" given by God?
> (Find answer from the first paragraph of Today's Message.)

> ### What is the consequence of adultery according to Proverbs 6:32?

> ### How does the love of money affect our lives?
> (1 Timothy 6:10)

APPLICATION

1. Reflect now and share – what is the actual impact of the fall of man on my own present life?

2. We have gone through three major consequences of the fall. If one of these shortcomings relates to you, share it with the Lord and repent of it now.

GOD PROMISED
REDEMPTION

INTRODUCTION

God hates sin but He loves the sinners. This tells us God is the God of love and the God of righteousness.

When the first man, Adam, hid from God because of his sin, God killed animals to cover this sinner's shame with its skins, and God covenanted that man would be redeemed through the coming Messiah. Beginning with His first covenant in Genesis 3:15, the words in the Old Testament give a full account of God's promises and covenants for His redemption work. He promised to Adam and Eve that "the child of the woman" would destroy Satan. Through His covenants with Noah, Abraham, and Abraham's children, the Passover lamb in Exodus, all the sacrifices in Leviticus and also through the prophecies of the Old Testament prophets, His promised work of redemption is spread throughout the Old Testament. All of His covenants and promises were perfectly fulfilled through Jesus' incarnation, death, and resurrection.

God Promised Redemption

17. The God of Righteousness and Love
18. God's Covenant of Salvation to Adam and Eve
19. God's Covenant to Noah
20. God's Covenant to the Patriarchs
21. The Passover Lamb and the Covenant of Redemption
22. The Covenant through Sacrifice
23. The Covenant through the Prophets

THE GOD OF RIGHTEOUSNESS AND LOVE

1. **Today's Scripture**
   1 John 4:7-12
2. **Memory Verse**
   1 John 4:8
   Whoever does not love does not know God, because God is love.
3. **Reference Scripture**
   Ezra 9:15
   John 3:16
4. **Objectives**
   a. Let us live in Jesus' love and share His love with others.
   b. Let us realize how righteous is the work of God and the provision of His redemptive work.
   c. Because of His great love, God sent even His only begotten Son, Jesus, to save us. Let us always give thanks to God.

LEADING QUESTIONS

> ### From where does love originate?
> (1 John 4:7-8)

> ### Why did God send His only begotten Son into the world?
> (1 John 4:14)

> ### If we love one another, what happens to God's love in us?
> (1 John 4:12)

TODAY'S MESSAGE

Many people think of God only as a strict and merciless judge who quickly judges us all the time. But our God is righteous and at the same time His love is boundless. He promised His redemption to us sinners, and fulfilled His promise by sending His Son. Nevertheless, fallen mankind does not know God as a good God. Through the Bible, let us know His righteousness and love that has been promised and fulfilled.

He is Righteous

God is righteous. Throughout human history, God revealed His righteousness most of the time through His judgements. The yardstick of His judgement has been His righteousness. No man is righteous when he stands before God. All mankind, and all things in the world too, have been judged since the first man Adam fell and was judged (Romans 5:12). Mankind cannot escape God's judgement and on the final judgement day everyone will be rewarded according to his deeds.

God judges each person fairly and thoroughly according to what he has done. In the Old Testament days, in order for the Israelites to escape God's severe judgement when they stood before Him, they had to shed the blood of animals, and this had to be repeated every time they committed sins. The shedding of the blood of animals symbolized the blood of Jesus Who was coming to shed His blood for the redemption of our sins. To stand before God, man must pay the price of his sins and the price of sin was death. In other words, man commits sins and to pay the price for sins, all who have sinned should die. But God did not want man to die for his own sins, so God sent His Son to die in man's place. That redeemer was Jesus Christ. When we believe in Jesus Christ and walk relying on the merits of His atoning work, we can rightfully stand before the righteousness of God just as if we'd never sinned.

By the help of Jesus' righteousness, when we arrive at God's righteousness, He stretches out His arms and protects us from Satan, enabling us to be more than conquerors over the evil power of the devil. This is possible because we became children of God through believing in the merits of the precious blood of Jesus Christ and obtaining eternal life.

He Is Love

God is love. The Trinity of God is love. Out of His love He created the heavens and the earth and all things therein. He created man also out of His love. Because God is love, He called out the fallen Adam and Eve, and "covered" them with the skins of animals that He killed, indicating that His redemption work would "cover" their sins.

In the Greek language, there are four words for love:

1. *Storge* – which generally tells about parental love
2. *Eros* – a love derived from physical gratification

3. *Philea* – a brotherly love
4. *Agape* – a love that gives out, or the sacrificial love of God.

God loves us to the point of giving Himself to us. God loves us not because He needs us but because we need His love.

Also, God's love is a one-way love. Just as Hosea forgave his adulterous wife because of his love for her, God called sin-committing Israel and also sent His Son to save His chosen children. Furthermore, God has loved us all along the way when we didn't even know Him.

Lastly, God's love is the love that gives and keeps on giving to all men. He not only loves His chosen children but He loves all of the world. God loves us just as we are. He loves us regardless of our circumstances. He love never changes, His love is the same yesterday, today and forever. He loves the sinful, the pious, the rich, the poor, thieves, prostitutes and all. The meaning of the scripture, *"God loved the world so much that he gave his only Son"* shows how great His love is.

How does God Give His Love to Us?

Because God loves us, He never forces us to make any decision but He leaves all things to our free will. Man, out of his own free will, chose to disobey God's Word and as a result of his rebellion he fell and became a sinner. Nevertheless, God still loved us and out of His love He sent His only Son, Jesus Christ, to pay the price of our sins. The Word of God declares this:

> *This is how God showed his love to us: He sent his only Son into the world to give us life through Him. True love is God's love for us, not our love for God. God sent his Son to be the way to take away our sins.* (1 John 4:9-10)

Being righteous, God does not overlook sin. Therefore to stand before God we should have paid the price of our sins. Jesus Christ was born by the miracle of a "virgin" birth by the power of the Holy Spirit. Because He was sinless He could pay the price of our sins. By His death, Jesus did pay the price of our sins and satisfied the righteousness of God. Not only did He pay the price of our sins, but whosoever believes in Him is saved and receives eternal life. This is a wondrous and amazing love to us. That Jesus shed blood on the cross, tells us how greatly God loves us.

We should not be content with just receiving this great love from God. In gratitude, we should show love one to another, and share with others the great love that called us and saved us when we were still in sin and without Christ.

> *That is how much God loved us, dear friends! So we also must love each other.* (1 John 4:11)

In other words, when we love each other with *agape* love, God's love comes and shines forth among us, which shows us God is in us and we are in Him. In order for us to love others in this way, we should commit ourselves totally to God, and that is only possible when we are really bathed in His great love. We must know how deeply and greatly our Heavenly Father loves us. To know this means we will practise His great love in all the events of our daily lives.

CLOSING QUESTIONS

> ### What were the reasons for God to choose and be pleased with the Israelites?
> (Deuteronomy 7:7-8)

> ### By sending Jesus Christ to the world, what did God want us to have?
> (John 3:16)

> ### How did God confirm that He loved us?
> (Romans 5:8)

APPLICATION

1 Let us totally rely on Jesus in all the aspects of our daily living.

2. Just as the waters of Galilee flow out of its borders, let us become those who let the love of God flow out from us to other people.

3. Let us give deep thanks to Jesus Christ for such a great love that He died on the cross to save us.

GOD'S COVENANT OF SALVATION TO
ADAM AND EVE

1. **Today's Scripture**
   Genesis 3:14-24
2. **Memory Verse**
   Genesis 3:15
   > *I will make you and the woman enemies to each other. Your descendants and her descendants will be enemies. Her child will crush your head. And you will bite his heel.*
3. **Reference Scripture**
   Romans 5:12-21
4. **Objectives**
   a. Let us believe Jesus Christ is our only Redeemer Who redeems us from sin and death.
   b. Our loving Heavenly Father gave us eternal life. Let us always be thankful to Him.

LEADING QUESTIONS

> **What were the punishments given by God in Genesis 3:16-17 to Adam and Eve respectively?**

> **In Genesis 3:15, who is the child of the woman?**
> (Galations 4:4)

> **What does the killing of animals to clothe Adam and Eve symbolize?**
> (Genesis 3:21)

TODAY'S MESSAGE

Succumbing to the temptation of Satan through the snake, our first parents, Adam and Eve, ate the fruit of the knowledge of good and evil and immediately sin, the curse and death came upon them. The moment sin entered into them, their spirits died and consequently their fellowship with God was broken. When God called Adam, he could not respond to God's voice nor come to God because he was too engulfed in shame to stand before Him. The wall of sin blocked the way of Adam's communion with God. We, the children of Adam, could not come forward to God either, nor respond to His merciful outstretched hands, because of our wall of sin.

But Jesus Christ came to this world and through his torn flesh and shed blood, He broke down the wall of sin that barred us from God. Jesus Christ Himself became the Way, the Truth and the Life. Through Him, the way opened for us to enter boldly the kingdom of God.

Many times and in many ways, the Bible prophesied the coming of Jesus Christ Who would be crucified in our place for sin. Let us study the first promise that God made with Adam and Eve.

The Promise of Redemption to Eve

Since Adam received directly from God the command not to eat the fruit of the tree of knowledge of good and evil, Satan chose Eve, who had not been told directly by God, and tempted her. First, Satan caused Eve to doubt God's goodness and led her to resent God's decision and grumble against Him. Soon, Eve took the fruit of the tree of knowledge of good and evil, ate of it and gave it to Adam to eat, and they were condemned. Now their spirits died and the curse which was placed on them was that they would earn their food by the sweat of their brow. For Eve, suffering in childbirth was added.

But our God is a God of love. His righteousness is tempered with love and mercy. God appeared to Adam and Eve and gave them a word of redemption. He said to the snake:
> *"I will make you and the woman enemies to each other. Your descendants and her descendants will be enemies. Her child will crush your head. And you will bite his heel."* (Genesis 3:15)

Here, the "child" was Jesus Christ, Who would destroy the head of the snake, Satan.

Why did God plan that Jesus Christ should be born of woman? The Psalmist David lamented:
> *I was brought into this world in sin. In sin my mother gave birth to me.* (Psalm 51:5)

Paul also sighed:
> *Sin came into the world because of what one man did. And with sin came death. And this is why all men must die – because all men sinned.* (Romans 5:12)

As the above scriptures declare, all men, no matter who they may be, born in sin because of Adam, are under the condemnation of original sin and by their own might it is possible for them to receive forgiveness from God or to escape judgement. Man fell by the act of his own free will but he is in no way capable of saving himself by the act of his own free will, because he became a servant of sin.

Therefore our Saviour, who was coming to deliver us from sin, could not come from the seed of man who was born through the sinful blood line of Adam. The Word of God prophesied plainly that our Saviour would be born of a virgin by the Holy Spirit:
> *But the Lord himself will give you a sign: The virgin will be pregnant. She will have a son and she will name him Immanuel.* (Isaiah 7:14)

The Fulfilment of the Promise by Jesus Christ

As prophesied, Jesus Christ was conceived of the virgin Mary by the Holy Spirit and was born as a sinless man, without the original sin that had been born into mankind generation after generation.

By disobeying God, Adam fell. By obeying God even to death, Jesus fulfilled God's will. Bound under original sin, no man was capable of keeping the laws, but Jesus obeyed the laws of God which were His thoughts all the time. The Apostle Paul wrote:
> *But when the right time came, God sent his Son. His Son was born of a woman and lived under the law. God did this so that he could buy freedom for those who were under the law. His purpose was to make us his children.* (Galations 4:4-5)

Whosoever believes in Jesus Christ will be cleansed by Jesus' blood, redeemed from the law and made a child of God.

At the same time, at the cross Jesus broke the power of Satan, and conquered death.
> *These children are people with physical bodies. So Jesus himself became like them and had the same experiences they have. He did this so that, by dying, he could destroy the one who has the power of death. That one is the devil.* (Hebrews 2:14)

One day, Satan will be bound and placed in the bottomless pit for a thousand years and then released for a short while. Eventually he will be cast into the lake of fire (Revelation chapter 20). Until that day Satan still has the power of the air and still comes to rob, kill and destroy people who do not know they can have victory over him. But the God of peace will crush Satan under our feet once and for all, shortly (Romans 16:20).

The Covenant and Fulfilment – Clothes of Animal Skins

When Adam and Eve had eaten of the forbidden fruit, they became aware of their nakedness and they became ashamed. When a person realizes he has sinned, the human tendency is to cover up the sin, so Adam and Eve began to do this. They made a covering for themselves – of fig leaves, but the leaves withered in time. Our own effort to cover up sin never lasts either.

When God came to talk with Adam and Eve, He took innocent animals, killed them, and with the skins of those animals He made a covering for both of them. The shedding of blood to provide this covering was a foreshadow of the coming of Jesus Who would shed His own blood to provide an everlasting covering for all sin, once and for all. Today, the only covering that can completely remove the shame and the guilt of man is the blood of Jesus Christ! No covering of human ethics or moral virtues can hide our shame and fear as a result of sin. Today "whosoever will" can be cleansed and made righteous only through the shed blood of Jesus.

As God promised through His Word, Jesus came to earth 2000 years ago. And when His atonement was completed, He declared, "*It is finished.*" (John 19:30) What did He finish? Our dead spirits were quickened. He delivered us from the curse of thorns and thistles. He redeemed us from the sickness that came as the wages of sin. This was the fulfilment of God's covenant made to Adam and Eve through His clothing them with animal skins.

We should live a life of thanksgiving to our Heavenly Father for His love and mercy, that we have eternal life through Jesus Christ.

CLOSING QUESTIONS

Who is the last Adam or the second man? **Where did He come from?** (1 Corinthians 15:45-49)

What has redeemed us from the useless life of our ancestors? (1 Peter 1:18-19)

The blood of Jesus has a better message than the blood of whom? (Hebrews 12:24)

Now consider the application of this lesson which you will find on the next page.

APPLICATION

1. Our Heavenly Father planned redemption for us from the very beginning, so He called us and redeemed us. Let us always give thanks to God for such a great and complete redemption.

2. Compare the difference between Jesus' and Adam's attitude toward God. Let us follow Jesus' model Who obeyed God all the way unto death, to become a peace offering sacrifice.

GOD'S COVENANT TO
NOAH

1. **Today's Scripture**
   Genesis 6:1-22
2. **Memory Verse**
   Genesis 6:22
   Noah did everything that God commanded him.
3. **Reference Scripture**
   Genesis 7:1-5
   Genesis 8:1-5
4. **Objectives**
   a. Let us be certain that those who believe in Jesus Christ shall live but those who do not believe in Jesus Christ shall die.
   b. Let us learn that if we enter the ark of faith we will always have sufficient faith to rise above the difficulties in our lives. Let us always live within the ark of faith and give thanks to God.

LEADING QUESTIONS

> ### Why was God sorry that He had made man on the earth?
> (Genesis 6:5-6)

> ### How did Noah appear to the Lord?
> (Genesis 6:8)

> ### How many days did it rain?
> (Genesis 7:4)

TODAY'S MESSAGE

Since Adam and Eve were cast out by God after their fall, all mankind became servants of Satan, who holds the power of the air today. However, God continually showed His plan of redemption towards man. Through Noah, whom God chose out of the sinful world of that day, God revealed His great truth of "salvation by faith" under His plan of grace. God also promised that His children would be saved through Jesus Christ, Who is the Ark of Salvation. Today, we will study the covenant that God made with Noah.

Man's Sin and God's Judgement

Just as God had promised, He blessed Adam and his offspring increased on the earth. But because they were born after Adam, they all entered the world as sinners too. Their thoughts were full of evil and rebellion against God. And people's relationships with one another were stained with hatred, hurts and murders.

After killing Abel, Cain and especially his descendants became even more wicked. Lamech, the fifth grandchild of Cain, was an extremely violent man. He killed a man who had wounded him and also killed a boy for injuring him. However, Seth was born to Adam after Abel was murdered and the children of Seth worshipped God diligently and walked with Him. Enoch, the fifth grandchild of Seth, walked with God for three hundred years and was taken up to heaven without experiencing death.

While the sons and daughters of Cain and Seth intermarried with one another, their wickedness increased. Iniquity filled the earth and God was deeply grieved. But in this whirlpool of wicked generations, there was a man who found favour with God and his name was Noah. He was a man with grace from God. His name meant "peace and comfort" and both overflowed in his life.

First, Noah was a righteous man before God. This does not mean that Noah was completely sinless before Him but it means that God reckoned him to be righteous because he trusted God and obeyed His words in faith.

Second, Noah was a good man. He was loyal to God, completely obeying God's Word and walking with Him.

Third, he found grace in the eyes of the Lord. Unless a person is pleasing in God's sight and has found grace, he cannot dare stand before God. Even though Noah was good and righteous in his every deed, if God had not given grace to him, his goodness and righteous acts would have been of no use.

To Noah, who enjoyed the grace of God as he walked with Him, God shared His plan of judgement on the wickedness of mankind, but He also showed Noah His plan of salvation from that judgement.

The Ark of Salvation Built by Faith

As God had commanded, Genesis built the ark of cypress wood. It was three storeys high, 135 metres long, 22.5 metres wide and 13.5 metres high.

To build this size of boat, a tremendous amount of wood, labour and working time, but most of all an unchanging faith in God's instructions, was required. While building the ark, Noah explained to people why he was building it. He also preached to them about the coming judgement of God and urgently invited them to come to the ark before the judgement began.

No one listened to Noah's preaching. Instead, they called him a crazy man. They made fun of him and ridiculed him when he finally gathered a male and a female of every kind of animal into the ark. Nevertheless, Noah believed firmly in God Who is faithful and he obeyed what he was told to do. Noah and his family not only believed God but lived accordingly. Through his faith he was recognized as a righteous man before God. Seeing that those aboard the ark were only the immediate family members of Noah, we can tell how scarce the humble men were in his days.

In time, the preparation period was over and the day of judgement arrived. As black clouds suddenly arose in the clear sky, sure enough rain drops began to fall just as God had warned, and Noah, his wife, and his three sons and three daughters-in-law got into the ark. The water began to rise. Higher and higher it rose until the ark floated over the high mountains. No doubt some of the people wanted to change their minds and enter the ark, but it was too late. All living creatures of the earth died. The rain continued for 40 days and for 150 days the earth was full of water. The ark that Noah had built by faith saved him and his family but that very same ark became proof of God's judgement to those who did not believe His words.

Noah's ark was God's covenant plan for saving those who would go into the ark. The ark was a foreshadow of the cross of Jesus Christ to mankind, that was destined to provide forgiveness of sins for all who would repent and ask for the cleansing blood of Jesus to remove their sins.

So, just as the ark was the way of salvation in the days of Noah, Jesus' shed blood on the cross is the way of salvation today from judgement to come. Today whosoever confesses Jesus as his personal Saviour will be forgiven his sins by Jesus' blood and he will be acquitted of future judgement.

Jesus' Ark of Salvation

Noah lived through the flood but he did not see the flood because the one window of the ark was open upwards to the sky. Noah could only look upwards so it was only the sky that Noah could see. Being in the ark, he could not even see a drop of rain, much less the flood. This is an important lesson to us who are already aboard Jesus' ark of salvation: "To be victorious during your flood, do not look at the flood." Instead of looking at the flood, open the window of prayer and look into God's face. Through prayer we can only see the faithfulness, grace and love of our heavenly Father. And through this window of prayer, let us build the altar of our prayer giving Him all praise and thanksgiving, and returning the glory to Him for all He has done for us.

What shall we do now, after we have boarded the ark of salvation and have obtained eternal life? We have the answer by looking at what Noah did after he came out of the ark. The first thing Noah did was to build an altar to God. There we can see him giving thanks to God for His salvation. Our God blesses the one who seeks His kingdom and His righteousness first, so He accepted Noah's altar and was pleased.

God blessed Noah with the words (Genesis 9:1):
"Have many children. Grow in number and fill the earth."
Noah did have many children. God also made a covenant with Noah. By placing a rainbow in the sky, God promised (Genesis 9:15):
"Flood waters will never again destroy all life on the earth."
That He would not judge all living creatures by water again, meant God had boundless love for the human race.

God has said He will judge the world by fire at the end of time. We are already aboard the ark of salvation, Jesus Christ, so we will not see judgement but we will be lifted up in the clouds to meet the Lord in the air.

CLOSING QUESTIONS

What is the way of salvation for my household and me?   (Acts 16:31)

In Noah's day, God judged the world by water. What will God use to judge the world at the end of time?   (2 Peter 3:6-10)

As the day of God approaches, what kind of people should we be?   (2 Peter 3:11-12)

APPLICATION

1. Compare today with Noah's day and realize the day of judgement is at hand. Let us persevere in our faith like Noah did.

2. When you are in a flood of problems which would try to discourage you, do not look at the flood, but look up only to your Heavenly Father and have fellowship with Him, knowing He will answer your prayer.

3. Let us have faith in the promise of God like Noah did.

GOD'S COVENANT TO
THE PATRIARCHS

1. **Today's Scripture**
   Genesis 12:1-3
2. **Memory Verse**
   Galatians 3:9
   All who believe today are blessed just as Abraham was blessed.
3. **Reference Scripture**
   Genesis 17:1-8
   Romans 9:6-13
4. **Objectives**
   a. We will learn that God established a covenant with Abraham,
      Isaac and Jacob and promised to send Jesus Christ to redeem
      us. Let us always give thanks to God for His love for us.
   b. Let us give thanks to God for His redemption that comes by
      His unconditional love, not by our works.

LEADING QUESTIONS

> **God promised "..... all the people on earth will be
> blessed through you."**
> **Who are "all the people on earth"?**
> (Genesis 12:3, Galations 3:8)

> **If we are children of faith, whose children have
> we become?**
> (Galations 3:7)

> **In Genesis 22:17, who would capture the
> cities of Abraham's enemies?**

TODAY'S MESSAGE

The divine providence for the redemption of mankind was
born out of God's love. It was not an improvisation. God
ordained it in the very beginning out of His great love that
always plans and fulfils the needs of mankind.

115

God revealed to Adam and Eve His plan of redemption, established that covenant of redemption through Noah's ark, and reassured His covenant to Abraham, Isaac and Jacob again and again.

Today, we will study God's covenant given to these three leaders of the Jewish tribes.

God's Covenant Made with Abraham

When God chose and called out Abraham, Abraham was living in fertile and flourishing Ur of the Chaldees near the Persian Gulf, where the Euphrates River and the Tigris River met.

God commanded him to leave his homeland and gave him four promises:

1. God would give him many descendants and they would become a great nation.
2. God would make his name great.
3. God would make him a great blessing.
4. Through Abraham, God would bless all other nations.

When Abraham left his native land and moved to Canaan, God fulfilled all the promises He had made with him. The fourth promise especially was fulfilled through a great miracle when Abraham became the father of Isaac at the age of 100. Isaac was to be the fulfilment of God's plan for Jesus Christ to be born through his lineage.

God promised Abraham:
"And I will make an agreement between me and you and all your descendants from now on. I will be your God and the God of all your descendants." (Genesis 17:7)
Here, God's covenant declared Abraham would become the father of many nations and exactly as the covenant stated, it came to pass. Abraham became the father of our faith and we became his children.

One day, God gave a shocking command to Abraham to offer Isaac as a burnt offering. But Abraham obeyed God's command in faith. When God saw his absolute total obedience and trust in Him, God commanded Abraham to halt and made certain of His covenant with him again:
"I will surely bless you and give you many descendants. They will be as many as the stars in the sky and the sand on the seashore. And they will capture the cities of their enemies. Through your descendants all the nations on the earth will be blessed. This is because you obeyed me." (Genesis 22:17-18)

116

If you look up these verses in the AV, you will see the word "seed" instead of "descendants" and this "seed" means Jesus Christ. Jesus became the "corn of wheat", that was buried, died and resurrected for us. He is the Holy Seed that never dies, through whom we are born again. Jesus Christ came to this world as the righteous seed to redeem all mankind and we too received the same life from Jesus when we believed and accepted Him in faith. The Apostle Paul declared this truth:

> If anyone belongs to Christ, then he is made new. The old things have gone; everything is made new. (2 Corinthians 5:17)

This blessing of redemption, whereby "everything is made new", came from the covenant that God had made with Abraham.

God's Covenant Established With Isaac

Isaac was a good man. He was meek and pious by nature. But God still demanded that Isaac be offered as a burnt offering. Without God's intervention, Isaac could have died by his father's knife. But God stopped Abraham and provided a ram.

All mankind without exception, no matter how meek and pure they may be and even if they have a temperament like Isaac, deserve death through the shedding of their blood for the wages of their sins. Isaac was a symbol of mankind under the power of sin and judgement too, but when God saw the faith of Abraham and Isaac, God sent a sacrificial offering of atonement for them.

Two thousand years after Isaac, Jesus Christ came to this world as the very Lamb of God that died on the cross in the place of Isaac and all mankind.

The land of Moriah, where Isaac had been bound, is located in Jerusalem. There, King Solomon built the House of the Lord where the blood of countless animals had been shed for the atonement of the people's sins. These sacrifices were a foreshadow of the coming of Jesus also, Who would shed His blood once and for all, for the price of our sins.

Through Isaac's experience, we are able to see how God established His covenant of redemption. Abraham called the name of the place "Jehovah-jireh", meaning "In the mount of the Lord, He provides." As shared above, when the fullness of time came, God provided the Ram of Atonement for our sins, Jesus Christ.

God also gave a prophetic promise to Isaac's wife Rebekah, that her descendants would capture the cities of the enemies (Genesis 24:60).

God's Foretelling of Redemption Through Jacob

With Abraham, God established a covenant for redemption. Through Isaac, He revealed how the redemption would be carried out. To Jacob He showed His sovereign right.

Jacob and Esau were twin brothers. While still in their mother's womb, God chose Jacob and established him as the seed for His covenant. This shows certainly that the decision for redemption came from God's grace and love and according to His sovereign choice, not from the things that man did, or by his nature or blood.

Jacob was a very greedy and deceitful man. In terms of moral conduct, he was not a bit better than Esau. But God loved Jacob to the extent that he put his hip out of joint in order to bring him to a place of repentance, and allowed him to enter the promised land by faith. When we see all this we know that our salvation is the gift from God to those who believe in His grace. The Word of God states:

All people have sinned and are not good enough for God's glory. People are made right with God by his grace, which is a free gift. They are made right with God by being made free from sin through Jesus Christ. (Romans 3:23-24)

So people receive God's promise by having faith. This happens so that the promise can be a free gift. And if the promise is a free gift, then all of Abraham's children can have that promise. The promise is not only for those people that live under the law of Moses. It is for anyone who lives with faith like Abraham. He is the father of us all. (Romans 4:16)

Our God is a good God who shared His plan of redemption and His covenant with us. As the Mediator of His covenant, Jesus Christ came. Therefore we should give thanks to God who brought us into His covenant, and invite all our family members and friends to come into this covenant also.

CLOSING QUESTIONS

> ### What made Abraham right with God?
> (Genesis 15:6)

> ### Romans 5:19 tells that by one man's obedience many will be made right with God. Who is this one man?

> ### If we are in faith with faithful Abraham, what will we receive?
> (Galatians 3:9)

APPLICATION

1. Let us hold fast the faith we received through God's salvation. All thanks, praise and honour are due our Heavenly Father for providing salvation.

2. We are all brothers and sisters in Jesus Christ, so let us love one another as Jesus loves us.

THE PASSOVER LAMB AND THE COVENANT OF REDEMPTION

1. **Today's Scripture**
   Exodus 12:1-4
2. **Memory Verse**
   Exodus 12:13
   But the blood will be a sign on the houses where you are. When I see the blood, I will pass over you. Nothing terrible will hurt you when I punish the land of Egypt.
3. **Reference Scripture**
   1 Corinthians 5:7-8
4. **Objectives**
   a. Let us give thanks to the Lord God Who revealed His redemptive plan to us through the Passover lamb.
   b. By studying the purpose of the Passover lamb for the Israelites' exodus, let us remember and understand what Jesus did for us believers. As we partake of His broken body and His shed blood, through the Lord's Supper, let us always strive to discipline ourselves to live a victorious life, knowing His crucifixion made our new life possible.

LEADING QUESTIONS

> ### Where did the Israelites kill the Passover lamb?
> (Exodus 12:1)

> ### Where did God command them to put the blood of the Passover lamb?
> (Exodus 12:7)

> ### What did God tell them that He would do that night?
> (Exodus 12:12)

TODAY'S MESSAGE

Twilight faded into evening shadows and night fell on the land of Goshen in Egypt. All of a sudden, shrieks of dying lambs were heard here and there and immediately the Israelites were busily putting the lamb's blood on the doorposts and above the door of each home, using hyssop dipped in the blood to strike the doorposts.

121

Quickly, all the community of the Israelites had followed their orders specifically. They had placed the blood of the lamb on all the doorposts and over the doors of each home, and every household was ready to set out for the long journey. Now they gathered together to eat their roasted lamb. Suddenly, at midnight, the whole country of Egypt was shaken by the wailing sounds of all the Egyptian families. Every household of Egypt from the palace of Pharaoh to the homes of the servants saw, at the same time, the death of their firstborn.

King Pharaoh now hurriedly called for Moses and told him to get out of the country quickly with the Israelites. Now, all the people of Israel, packed and ready to leave, set out for the promised land, Canaan, leaving behind at last the foreign land where they had been enslaved for 430 long years.

Enslaved Mankind

The lamb killed for the Passover in Egypt was a foreshadow of Jesus Christ. In partaking of communion together, we look back to the great day of deliverance for the Israelites, which came as they partook of the lamb according to the instructions which were given. After believing in Jesus Christ as our Saviour, through the elements which remind us of His torn flesh and His shed blood, we too partake of new life by faith, healing by faith and everything we need to be victorious for Him! John the Baptist told about this in John 1:29:
"Look, the Lamb of God. He takes away the sins of the world!"
Through the miraculous work of the Passover we can see clearly God's sheer determination to deliver mankind from the bondage of Satan's slavery, through the power of Jesus' sacrificial death for you and me.

In his original state of creation, man was a free and noble being, just as Jacob and his seventy family members were free and noble when they first entered the land of Egypt. Jacob's whole household were treated as royal guests of the Egyptian king Pharaoh, because the king had successfully overcome severe famine with the help of Joseph's wise counsel. For this reason, the king settled them in the land of Goshen.

But the children of Jacob, living in Egypt generation after generation, forgot about their God and followed the Egyptians' lifestyle, eventually indulging in idol worship. They had forsaken their God, the God of Abraham, Isaac and Jacob, and punishment from God had followed in the form of oppression by the Egyptian king.

Time passed and the king who favoured Joseph died, and Joseph died too. A new king who did not know Joseph came to power. He did not like the Israelites multiplying and becoming strong. He made all of the Israelites his servants and persecuted them by killing every Jewish boy born at birth. He intended to exterminate every descendant of the Israel race.

If we see this persecution through the window of our spiritual eyes, it is the same as it was when we became servants to Satan, when Adam and Eve fell. Since the devil's business is *to steal and kill and destroy*" (John 10:10) all of mankind, the servants of the devil now fell into the state of dying, spiritually and physically, being stripped of their joy, peace and health to the extent of being destroyed by the devil.

But God wanted to save His suffering children from the bondage of slavery. In the light of God's righteousness and justice, all sinners deserve death just as the firstborn child of each Egyptian family received death, but God, through His Son's redemptive work, forgave our sins, transferred us from death and delivered us from the slavery of sin. God set us free. Let us now study how the blood and flesh of Jesus, our Passover, set us free.

The Blood of Jesus Christ

The Bible clearly states:
> *All people have sinned and are not good enough for God's glory.* (Romans 3:23)

Jesus came to this world as the sinless Redeemer to bear our sin in our place. By shedding His blood, He once and for all removed our sin, unrighteousness, curse and despair. Jesus died as the Passover lamb to buy back all of us from every race, language and nation, and to give us to God (Revelation 5:9). Jesus' blood is so precious that for the price of His blood, our lives could be redeemed back to God.

The blood of Jesus also established a covenant, or agreement, between God and us (1 Corinthians 11:25). And by this covenant whosoever believes in Jesus as his personal Saviour will receive eternal life and salvation (John 3:16).

Furthermore, Jesus' blood is the sin-forgiving blood. Because we are weak, we commit sin occasionally. But when we confess our sins to the Lord Jesus Christ, relying on His blood, we will be forgiven. The peace and joy of being forgiven by our Lord comes to us and we gradually learn to live a clean life by depending more on the Lord.

The blood of Jesus has the power to make us righteous and lead us to the way of sanctification. By the blood of Jesus we also enter into peace with God.

Jesus' blood is powerful enough to change the vilest sinner. On the merits of His blood, we can always come forward to God and pray. Through His blood, He always helps us to live a victorious Christian life.

Therefore, we must always put the blood of Jesus over the entrance of our heart. Plead the blood of Jesus over your life – your home, your work for God and every area of your daily living. When we rely on His blood, all the blessing, power and victory from God comes to help us. In order for us to apply the blood of Jesus to our hearts we should sing about His blood, recognize its power, and give thanks to the Lord through our mouth in confession.

The Flesh of Jesus Christ

The Israelites in Egypt not only put the blood of the Passover lamb on both sides of the door and on the lintel but they also ate all of the Passover lamb.

The meat of the Passover lamb signifies the **body of Jesus**, as the Lord Jesus stated in John 6:51:
> *"I am the living bread that came down from heaven. If anyone eats this bread, he will live forever. This bread is my flesh. I will give my flesh so that the people in the world may have life."*

The meat of the Passover lamb also means the **Word of God**. Jesus Christ dwells in us as God's Word that came in flesh. Just as the children of Israel ate the meat and obtained the necessary strength to travel through the wilderness en route to Canaan, we too should "eat" the Word of God to obtain strength to live through this wilderness of life.

When we eat the Word of God we are also cleansed as Jesus taught His disciples:
> *"You are already clean because of the words I have spoken to you. Remain in me ...."* (John 15:3-4)

In the Word of God there is healing power! God heals us by His Word and also helps us out when we are in trouble. As we eat God's Word along the way, we are able to learn to make wise decisions in life and our inner person grows day by day. The scripture also states:
> *We are healed because of his wounds.* (Isaiah 53:5; 1 Peter 2:24)

As He hung on the cross and bore our curse He set us free from the bondage of that curse. Our spirit, soul and body are born again through His sacrificial death for us.

Today we have learned that the Passover lamb of Exodus signifies Jesus Christ, Who saves all mankind from the slavery of the devil and sin. It is the same today. By applying Jesus' blood on the doorposts of our heart, eating of His broken body, and living on the Word of God, we are able to enjoy true freedom and abundant life, freed from the shackles of the devil.

CLOSING QUESTIONS

> ### Whose sin did Jesus take away?
> (John 1:29)

> ### What did God specifically require of the Israelites in order that they would not be destroyed with the Egyptians?
> (Exodus 12:13)

> ### How many days did the Israelites keep the Passover lamb in the house?
> (Exodus 12:3-6)

APPLICATION

1. Let us give thanks to our Heavenly Father who revealed to us His redemptive plan via the Passover lamb. Let us witness this love of God to unbelieving friends.

2. Let us claim the blood of Jesus in our household and lead all our family members to the road of deliverance from the power of sin and judgement. Let us teach them about God's forgiveness.

3. Let us always meditate on the Word of God and eat it as our meal.

THE COVENANT THROUGH
SACRIFICE

1. **Today's Scripture**
   Hebrews 10:1-18
2. **Memory Verse**
   Hebrews 10:10
   > *Jesus Christ did what God wanted him to do. And because of this, we are made holy through the sacrifice of his body. Christ made this sacrifice only once, and for all time.*
3. **Reference Scripture**
   Leviticus chapters 1 - 6
   Hebrews 7:27
   Hebrews 9:11-14
4. **Objectives**
   a. Let us study what kind of sacrifices were offered to God in Old Testament days and the meaning of each type of sacrifice.
   b. Let us study how these sacrifice offerings relate to the redemption work of Jesus Christ.

LEADING QUESTIONS

> **Because of the once-and-for-all sacrifice of Jesus Christ, what kind of efforts were eliminated on our part?**
> (Hebrews 7:27)

> **To make their bodies clean, what did the people of the Old Testament do?**
> (Hebrews 9:13)

> **Through the offering of His body once and for all, what did Jesus do specifically for us?**
> (Hebrews 10:10)

TODAY'S MESSAGE

L eviticus is the most minutely written account of all the laws concerning sacrifices and offerings which were observed by the Israelites. The book of Leviticus is like a picture book that God Himself would draw and use in religious training for His own children. All the picture types in Leviticus point ahead to the coming Jesus Christ.

One of the most fundamental questions for mankind is how an unholy man may approach the Holy God. The Bible clearly answers: to come to God one must bring a sacrifice offering. We all, without any exception, know deep down in our hearts that we are helpless sinners. That is why even the pagans, knowing they cannot solve their sin problem by their own might, bring sacrifices whenever they serve their gods. These kinds of sacrifices are nothing but vain sacrifices to their lifeless gods. But the sacrifices and offerings as recorded in Leviticus were a foreshadow, a type, behind which our Lord Jesus Christ was standing as our once-and-for-all sacrifice, to be offered at Calvary's Hill to make atonement for all the sins of mankind. All the religious ceremonies for God in the Old Testament point to

......the Lamb of God. He takes away the sins of the world!
(John 1:29)

Today, let us study together how the five sacrifices and offerings recorded in Leviticus foreshadow the redeeming work of our Saviour Jesus Christ which was to come.

The Burnt Offering (Leviticus chapter 1)

A "burnt offering" originally meant "going up" because it goes up to the altar to be offered. This burnt offering was mentioned more than all other sacrifices as it was the first and most generally offered sacrifice.

Most of the time the sacrifice was of male livestock but in some instances turtledoves or young pigeons were acceptable. The order was as follows: the offerer put his hand on the head of the burnt offering, killed it on the north side of the altar before the Lord, cut the sacrifice animal into pieces, and washed the inner organs and the legs with water. The officiating priest then sprinkled its blood all around on the altar and burned all the sacrifice on the altar.

During significant feast seasons they offered the burnt sacrifices in the morning and evening of the day. The important meaning of the ceremony of the burnt offering lies in the perfect consecration and dedication of the one offering it, as Paul teaches in Romans 12:1:

.... offer your lives as a living sacrifice to him. Your offering must be only for God and pleasing to him.

The burnt offering foreshadows Jesus Christ Who gave Himself without blemish to God. Jesus Christ sacrificed His life totally as the sin offering in our stead.

The Grain Offering (Leviticus chapter 2)

The "grain offering" could be offered together with other animal sacrifices. Grains which were offered included fine flour, unleavened baked pan bread or grain from the first harvest. On the altar, the priest burned a handful of the grain offering that had salt, oil or incense added and the remaining of the grain offering was given to the priest. If the priest was the one offering the sacrifice, he burned the whole grain offering.

Usually, rich people gave the grain offering in addition to the burnt sacrifice or peace offering (Numbers 15:25-26) and the poor offered only the grain offering. The grain offering was a daily offering foreshadowing Christ's serving life. The fine flour represented Christ's characteristics, His perfect nature.

The Fellowship or Peace Offering (Leviticus chapter 3)

As the name indicates, the fellowship offering (or peace offering in the AV) was literally a sacrifice for peace and fellowship with God. The thanksgiving offering, vow offering and the voluntary offering all belonged to the peace offering. The thanksgiving offering was generally for giving thanks to the Lord God because the offerer had already received blessings. The vow offerings were given in expectation of blessings coming in the future. Voluntary offerings were extra offerings given willingly with the offerer's prayer request, and they were not a condition for blessings.

For the peace offering, either male or female animals were acceptable and were given together with unleavened cakes of fine flour mingled with oil. This peace sacrifice symbolizes the peace of Jesus Christ.

> *For he is our peace, who hath made both one, and hath broken down the middle wall of partition between us.* (Ephesians 2:14 AV)

> *God made peace by using the blood of Christ's death on the cross.* (Colossians 1:20)

The Sin Offering (Leviticus 4:1-5:13)

If the Israelites sinned against any of God's commandments, they offered a sin offering (Leviticus 4:2-3). When a person did not respond to being summoned as a witness, when he touched unclean things which were against their laws, when he carelessly made a vow, or unintentionally committed any sins, he was required to offer a sin offering.

One thing to note, in the case of a sin offering, is that the sacrificer came to the altar of God as a sinner, with an attitude of acknowledging and repenting of his sins. He did not come as a worshipper, as in the case of other sacrifices, but stood before God as a sinner. In other words, God, through our sin offering sacrifice, placed man in the position where he realized his responsibility for the sins he had committed. When the offerer offered the sin offering, he stood before the presence of God as a criminal stands before the judge in a court. All of his sins were atoned for by the blood of his sin-substitute animal. So this sin offering was a foreshadow of the death of Jesus when He would shed His blood to make atonement for all our sins. Therefore the sacrifice of the sin offering represents the redeeming death of Jesus Christ, our Saviour.

The Trespass Offering (Leviticus 5:14-6:7 AV)

The nature and meaning of the trespass offering was similar to the sin offering. It was offered generally when a person had committed sin against his neighbours and had to make restitution for a loss. For anything deceitfully obtained, or harmed, the person was to give the full value back, plus an additional one-fifth, according to Leviticus 6:5. The sinner was forgiven and the victim also was recompensed.

First of all, the significance of the trepass offering is that Jesus Christ not only bore our sins against God but He also bore the sins we committed against others. And if we come to Him with our sins He will always forgive us because of His great mercy.

We have reviewed the five kinds of sacrifices and offerings in the Old Testament and how they were a foreshadow of the redeeming work of Jesus Christ.

In the fullness of time, Jesus Christ was born and perfectly fulfilled all the laws about sacrifices and offerings in Leviticus, by giving Himself to God as the sacrificial lamb without spot or blemish. Shedding the blood of sacrifice animals, as the Israelites did, is no longer needed. By being our sin substitute, Jesus Christ once and for all perfected the work of redemption.

CLOSING QUESTIONS

> ### What kind of sacrifice offerings were required in Old Testament days?
> (Find answer from today's message.)

> ## The Old Testament sacrifices pointed to whom?
> (John 1:29)

> ## What happened when Jesus was offered as our fellowship or peace offering?
> (Ephesians 2:14)

APPLICATION

1. Ponder deeply how the five sacrifice offerings of the Old Testament are related to you personally.

2. Share with one another any points on which you have been enlightened or blessed from today's message.

THE COVENANT THROUGH THE
PROPHETS

1. Today's Scripture
   Isaiah 53:1-12

2. Memory Verse
   Isaiah 53:5

   But he was wounded for the wrong things we did. He was crushed for the evil things we did. The punishment which made us well, was given to him. And we are healed because of his wounds.

3. Reference Scripture
   Isaiah 7:14
   Isaiah 61: 1-2

4. Objectives
   a. Our Heavenly Father promised through His chosen prophets that He would send our Saviour Jesus and He fulfilled His promise. Let us give thanks to God for sending Jesus to redeem us.
   b. Let us also live in the blessed hope and faith that Jesus will return again to the earth, as promised by God.

LEADING QUESTIONS

> ### Who is "he" in Isaiah 53:1-3?

> ### Whose suffering and pain did He take on Himself?
> (Isaiah 53:4)

> ### To what was He likened when He remained silent during His suffering?
> (Isaiah 53:7)

TODAY'S MESSAGE

Seven hundred years before Jesus was born on this earth, Isaiah prophesied that He would come and would be crucified on the cross for the wrong and evil things we had done. In planning to redeem mankind, God let this plan of His love be known in advance. Today, we will study the prophecies concerning this plan, and their fulfilment, through several scriptures.

The Prophecy and Fulfilment of Jesus' Birth

God foretold in the Bible, in detail, the place, time and setting of Jesus' birth.   When moved upon by the Holy Spirit, the prophet Micah, a contemporary of Isaiah and Hosea, who lived 700 years before Christ, prophesied where Jesus would be born (Micah 5:2) and Jesus was actually born as told, in Bethlehem, 7 kilometres from Jerusalem (Luke 2:4, 5, 7).   Around BC 600, Daniel, captive in Babylonia, prophesied Jesus' coming (Daniel 9:25).   As prophesied, Jesus came to this world and was crucified.   God also said that Jesus would be born as "the seed of woman," of a virgin, without a natural father (Isaiah 7:14), and He was really born of the virgin, Mary (Luke 1:26, 27, 30, 31).   The Apostle Paul witnesses to this in Galatians 4:4-5:

> *But when the right time came, God sent his Son. His Son was born of a woman and lived under the law. God did this so that He could buy freedom for those who were under the law. His purpose was to make us his children.*

Hosea 11:1, *"calling my son out of Egypt"*, was a prophecy that Jesus and His family would go to Egypt for a while to escape from the persecution of Herod (Matthew 2:14-15).

As we shared above, God prophesied the birth of Jesus through His chosen servants and Jesus came, just as it was prophesied through the prophets.

The Ministry of Jesus

One thousand years before Jesus came to this world, David, moved upon by the Holy Spirit, prophesied in Psalm 2:7:

> *Now I will tell you what the Lord has declared: He said to me "You are my son. Today I have become your father."*

And when Jesus was baptized in water the heavens opened and a voice was heard:

> *"This is my Son and I love him. I am very pleased with him."* (Matthew 3:17)

After His water baptism, Jesus taught in Galilee as prophesied (Isaiah 9:1-2, Matthew 4:12-16). The word that Jesus taught means He carried out His ministry as a prophet and this was also foretold by Moses:

> *The Lord your God will give you a prophet like me. He will be one of your own people. Listen to him.* (Deuteronomy 18:15)

Here the "prophet" meant Jesus (Acts 3:20-22).

Jesus' Messianic ministry of telling the good news to the poor, declaring freedom to the captive, announcing God's forgiveness, was all prophesied through Isaiah (Isaiah 61:1-2, Luke 4:18-19). His being rejected was also foretold in Isaiah 53:3.

Jesus became our eternal High Priest (Hebrews 3:1, 5:5-6, 7:1-3) as declared in Psalm 110:4:

> *You are a priest forever, a priest like Melchizedek.*

When Jesus entered Jerusalem on a donkey He was praised as a king and this was mentioned in Zechariah 9:9.

Jesus Christ came to this world as prophesied in the Word of God and He fulfilled all the prophecies concerning Him as a Prophet, Priest and King.

Jesus' Suffering and Resurrection

David prophesied Jesus' betrayal:

> *My best and truest friend ate at my table. Now even he has turned against me.* (Psalm 41:9)

On the night of the last Passover feast, Jesus told Judas:

> *"The thing that you will do – do it quickly!"* (John 13:27)

and

> *"Judas, are you using the kiss to give the Son of Man to his enemies?"* (Luke 22:48)

As prophesied in Zechariah 11:12, Jesus was sold for thirty pieces of silver (Matthew 26:15).

Though He was accused falsely by witnesses (Psalm 35:11, Mark 14:57-58) He remained silent (Isaiah 53:7). As prophesied, people spat at, mocked and hit Jesus (Isaiah 50:6) and hated him without cause (Psalm 35:19).

Jesus died as our sin substitute (Isaiah 53:5) and the Apostle Paul states this in Romans 5:6:

> *Christ died for us while we were still weak. We were living against God, but at the right time Christ died for us.*

Isaiah 53:12 told that He was treated like a criminal and He was in fact hung between two thieves (Mark 15:27-28).

Zechariah prophesied his stabbing (Zechariah 12:10) and in John 20:27 Jesus told His disciple Thomas to touch His pierced side. Jesus Christ received all kinds of insult and mockery as Psalm 22 states.

Giving Jesus vinegar was also prophesied in Psalm 69:21, and His prayer on the cross (Luke 23:34) was in Psalm 109:4:

"Father forgive them. They don't know what they are doing."
Lots being cast for his clothes (Psalm 22:17-18), His bones remaining unbroken (Psalm 34:20), His burial in a rich man's tomb (Isaiah 53:9) were all prophesied and actually happened as told.

David also prophesied:
> *....you will not leave me in the grave. You will not let your holy one rot.* (Psalm 16:10)
> *But God will save my life. He will take me from the grave.* (Psalm 49:15)

His ascension was also prophesied in Psalm 68:18.

As we have shared above, Jesus' birth, ministry, suffering, crucifixion, resurrection and ascension were all prophesied. And the New Testament witnesses to the fulfilment of all these prophecies.

When we study these prophecies and their exact fulfilment, we cannot help but praise God and give thanks to Him that the planned redemption was thoroughly and faithfully accomplished.

CLOSING QUESTIONS

Read Isaiah 53:5-6:
Why was Jesus wounded?
Why was Jesus crushed?
Why was Jesus punished?
How was Jesus treated?
(Isaiah 53:12)

1 Our Heavenly Father is faithful and He certainly answers our prayer when we have faith in His Word of promise.

2. When we witness to Jesus it would be very powerful if we compared the prophetic words in the Old Testament with their actual fulfilment in the New Testament.

GOD BECAME
MAN

INTRODUCTION

This unit deals with Christology. Who is Jesus Christ? He is the fulfiller of God's covenants. Jesus is God who became man. He is truly God and He is truly human. He exists before time and eternally. He came to this earth about 2,000 years ago clothed in human flesh, lived for 33 years, died, was resurrected and ascended back to heaven. The purpose of His coming was to save God's chosen children from sin. He fulfilled this purpose through His crucifixion and resurrection. His representative offices were Prophet, Priest and King of kings and He accomplished all His jobs fully through His perfect love, meekness and humility. Let us now understand clearly by studying the following lessons that the Saviour is "My Jesus" and witness to Him powerfully to our neighbours as "Your Jesus".

God Became Man

WHO IS
JESUS CHRIST?

1. **Today's Scripture**
   Matthew 16:13-20
2. **Memory Verse**
   Matthew 16:15-16
   > *Then Jesus asked them, "And who do you say I am?" Simon Peter answered, "You are the Christ, the Son of the living God."*
3. **Reference Scripture**
   Matthew 1:18-25
   Luke 1:26-38
4. **Objectives**
   a. Let us always be prepared to answer correctly when anyone asks, "Who is Jesus Christ?"
   b. Let us know who Jesus is to us and walk in Him always.

LEADING QUESTIONS

> ### In the matter of Jesus' birth, how did His birth differ entirely from ours?
> (Matthew 1:18)

> ### What is the meaning of "Jesus"?
> (Matthew 1:21)

> ### What is the other name of Jesus Christ and its meaning?
> (Matthew 1:23)

TODAY'S MESSAGE

When Jesus was in Caesarea Philippi with his disciples, He asked them, *"Who do the people say I am?"* The disciples reported that people said Jesus was John the Baptist, or Elijah, or one of the prophets. Then Jesus asked His disciples again, *"And who do you say I am?"* Simon Peter answered, *"You are the Christ, the Son of the living God."* And Jesus highly commended Peter for his confession of faith.

Even today, a great many people recognize Jesus as a great teacher

139

or one of the prophets at the most. They think Jesus is just one of the extraordinary men in history who suddenly came and disappeared. But this is not true.

Jesus, though He is God, came to this earth in order to become the Lamb of Sacrifice offering to die for the sins of mankind.

He was conceived of the Holy Spirit and born of the virgin Mary. There was no other plan. This incarnation of Jesus Christ was not an accident that happened out of a vacuum. Christ's coming was planned long before His incarnation. Then who is this Jesus Christ indeed? We will find the answer this time by going through the scripture and finding out the historical facts about Him.

Jesus is the Promised Messiah Who was Prophesied in the Holy Scriptures

Already in Genesis, God promised that the Messiah would come to this earth. Mankind's first parents Adam and Eve fell under Satan's rule after their sin and they were separated from God. But God did not want mankind to perish, so He promised to send the Messiah to destroy the work of the devil. This promised Messiah, described in the AV as the "seed of woman", is Jesus Christ. Jesus as the seed of woman signifies that He would be conceived by the Holy Spirit and be born through a virgin, whereas all other men are born from the seed of man.

God also told through the prophet Micah the exact location where the Messiah would be born (Micah 5:2), that is, Bethlehem in the land of Judea. Through the prophet Isaiah, God prophesied the Messiah is truly human and truly God and He would be the Saviour of mankind (Isaiah 9:6).

Psalm 22 and Isaiah chapter 53 delineate in great detail the suffering of Christ, His becoming our sin offering and what blessings we will receive through His death in our stead.

Jesus Christ's coming as our Saviour was prophesied progressively throughout the 4,000 years of history in the Old Testament. God told us through these prophecies how Jesus would come, minister, suffer and die. In His providence, God preordained Christ to come, and also revealed through His prophecies in the Bible that we would certainly know He is indeed the promised Messiah.

Jesus Christ is the Central Point of the Chronicle of History

The coming of Jesus Christ divides annals that we use now: Before Christ (B.C.) and After Christ (or Anno Domini). Also the 66 books of the Bible, Genesis, through to Revelation, write the human history. The opening of the Bible, Genesis, records the origin of the universe and the last book, Revelation, speaks about the end time. In other words, the Word of God includes all things about the very beginning and the very end of the history of the world and its theme is Jesus Christ. The thing we could not possibly overlook is that some 40 odd writers recorded these 66 books throughout a period of some 1,600 years and, miraculously, the unchanging theme is Jesus Christ. What does this mean? It means that Jesus Christ is the central figure of all history, from eternity to eternity. Therefore, those who do not walk in union with Jesus Christ can never understand the flow of history, nor live rightly.

Jesus Christ is God Who Became Man

Why did God become man? Why did He need to be in the flesh and of human nature? Why had he gone through the process of incarnation? This is the question leading to the purpose of His incarnation and we can approach the answer as follows:

First, **to reveal God the Father**. No man has seen the invisible God. Jesus came to this world to reveal to us who God is. Being in Jesus, we know the nature and character of God, and knowing Jesus we know God. In addition, through Jesus' perfect living and redemptive death, we are enlightened of God's plan towards us.

Second, **to atone for our sins by the sacrifice of Himself**. We are all sinners and thus are destined to death. But God provided the way to take the condemnation which was due to us, onto Himself. It was the only way to save us. Therefore, Jesus needed to come in the flesh to become the wage of our sin on the cross in our stead. To become man's Saviour, Jesus came as man.

Third, **to be a mediator**. Because of man's sin, committed from the beginning, man's way of having fellowship with God was cut off. The wall and the impassable deep valley of sin lies between the sinners and the Holy God. But God wanted to break the barrier and provide a way for the fallen man to return to Him. Through His torn flesh and shed blood on the cross, Jesus Christ became the bridge connecting God and man, and via Jesus we received the grace to become God's children.

As we have gone through the above, we see the reason for Jesus' incarnation was "to seek and to save one that was lost".

CLOSING QUESTIONS

Who is Jesus Christ?
(Matthew 16:15-16)

At various times, the Old Testament promised to send the Messiah into the world.
Draw a line between each of the following verses and its content.

Genesis 3:15	Saviour Who is truly God, truly man
Micah 5:2	Seed of woman
Isaiah 9:6	Place where He will be born

What does Jesus' crucifixion bring about for us?
(Ephesians 2:14-16)

1. Let us engrave on our heart, one more time, Who Jesus is and what He has done for us.

2. Let us live a life that truly witnesses about Jesus' love to others.

JESUS CHRIST IS
GOD

1. **Today's Scripture**
   John 1:1-3
2. **Memory Verse**
   John 1:1
   Before the world began, there was the Word. The Word was with God, and the Word was God.
3. **Reference Scripture**
   Isaiah 9:6
   John 10:29-30
4. **Objectives**
   a. Let us learn that Jesus is the Son of God.
   b. Let us experience in our lives that Jesus Christ is truly God, and confess this truth.

LEADING QUESTIONS

> ### What did John the Baptist call Jesus Christ?
> (John 1:1)

> ### Since when does Jesus exist and with whom?
> (John 1:2)

> ### Who made all things of the universe?
> (John 1:3)

TODAY'S MESSAGE

Though He is God, Jesus Christ came to this world to rescue sinners who are death-bound. Jesus paid the price of our sins by His death on the cross. He bestowed on us this amazing love and today we will study this Jesus Who is truly God.

Jesus is the Same as His Father

Many doctrinal heresies about the person of Jesus Christ emerged during the early church period. Among the heretics were the Gnostics. Their teaching was a perversion of the gospel, adopting Greek philosophy to interpret the scripture. This Hellenistic view

143

upheld the teaching that all flesh or material is evil and all the spirit or soul is good. Influenced by this philosophy, the Gnostics spread a heresy that denied the deity of Christ. They questioned how a good God could possibly come in the flesh that they thought to be evil. The church began to fight this heresy and that is why the Apostle John emphasized the deity of Jesus Christ in the gospel of John and his other epistles. In 325 AD, the church adopted a statement about the deity of Jesus known as the Nicene Creed, the first part of which reads as follows:

> I believe in one God
> the Father almighty,
> maker of heaven and earth,
> and of all the things visible and invisible:
>
> And in one Lord Jesus Christ,
> the only-begotten Son of God,
> begotten of his Father before all worlds,
> God of God, Light of Light,
> very God of very God,
> begotten, not made,
> being of one substance with the Father,
> by whom all things were made;
> who for us men and for our salvation
> came down from heaven,
> and was incarnate by the Holy Ghost
>   of the Virgin Mary,
> and was made man,
> and was crucified also for us
>   under Pontius Pilate.
> He suffered and was buried,
> and the third day he rose again
> according to the scriptures,
> and ascended into heaven,
> and sitteth on the right hand of the Father.
> And he shall come again with glory
> to judge both the quick and the dead:
> whose kingdom shall have no end . . .

Evidence that Jesus Christ is Truly God

The Bible witnesses that Jesus Christ is God.

First, Jesus is God because He possesses all the attributes of deity – omnipotence, eternal self-existence, omnipresence, immutability and so on. Jesus is as truly God as God the Father and God the Holy Spirit.

144

Second, the phenomenon of Jesus' birth declares He is truly God. Jesus was conceived by the Holy Spirit which means He came to this world by God's supernatural and divine method, not by natural and human ways. He came as prophesied (Isaiah 7:14, Matthew 1:18) through a virgin, without a natural father. This miracle of conception would never have been possible if He had not been the Son of God. Also the Prophet Isaiah foretold exactly that the coming baby, Jesus Christ, would be Almighty God (Isaiah 9:6).

Third, Jesus Himself witnessed that He is truly God in John 10:29-30:

> *"My Father gave my sheep to me. He is greater than all, and no person can steal my sheep out of my Father's hand. The Father and I are One."*

The Apostle Paul stated Jesus to be in the form of God (Philippians 2:6). The writer of Hebrews also witnessed clearly that Jesus

> *... reflects the glory of God. He is an exact copy of God's nature.* (Hebrews 1:3)

Fourth, all the miracles that Jesus performed during His ministry witnessed that Jesus is truly God. He changed water to wine. He fed 5,000 people from five loaves and two fish. He calmed the sea, walked on the water, healed the sick, cast out the devil, raised the dead and the like. Jesus spoke Himself:

> *"I do miracles in my Father's name. Those miracles show who I am."* (John 10:25)

> *"The Father and I are one."* (John 10:30)

Jesus repeated in John 10:37-38 about His deity:

> *"If I don't do what my Father does, then don't believe me. But if I do what my Father does, even though you don't believe in me, believe what I do. Then you will know and understand that the Father is in me and I am in the Father."*

Doing all the miraculous works in the name of God, Jesus testified to that fact that He and God are one.

Lastly, Jesus' resurrection and ascension prove that He is God. In human history, no man has ever been resurrected from the dead. Not one single soul has ever broken the power of the grave and death. But our Lord Jesus Christ overcame the power of death, was resurrected in three days and ascended into heaven as His disciples were watching (Luke 24:51, Acts 1:9). This incident lucidly witnesses to the deity of Jesus as Paul aptly states in Romans 1:4:

> *....through the Spirit of holiness he was appointed to be God's Son with great power by rising from death.*

As the disciple Thomas confessed "my Lord and my God" we too should believe in Jesus Christ as our God.

Jesus' Eternal Deity

The Apostle Paul said of Jesus:

> *No one has seen God but Jesus is exactly like him. Christ ranks higher than all the things that have been made.* (Colossians 1:15)

Then does this mean that Jesus was the first being created by God? Or does it mean that there is a distinctive beginning of His deity? According to the gospel of John, Jesus Christ was with God in the beginning (John 1:2). Jesus Himself said:

> *"You people are from here below. But I am from above. You belong to this world but I don't belong to this world."* (John 8:23)

In John 3:13 Jesus revealed that He came from heaven where He had been and also said that He existed even before Abraham (John 8:58), which proves He was with God in the beginning.

Jesus prayed: *"And now, Father, give me glory with you. Give me the glory I had with you before the world was made."* (John 17:5)

This word of Jesus Himself underscores the eternal deity of Jesus Christ.

Our Lord Jesus Christ is truly God:

> *The Lord God says, "I am the Alpha and the Omega. I am the One who is and was and is coming. I am the All-Powerful."* (Revelation 1:8)

CLOSING QUESTIONS

What did Jesus say about Himself?
(John 10:30)

List the three points of evidence from the following verses that Jesus Christ was not the first creature of God:
   a. John 1:2
   b. John 8:58
   c. John 17:5

Now consider the application of this lesson which you will find on the next page.

APPLICATION

1. We are the ones who should have paid the price of our sin and hung on the cross. But Jesus paid it for us. Let us share again His great love towards us, and give deep thanksgiving to Him.

2. Share with one another any new insights gained from today's message.

JESUS CHRIST IS
MAN

1. **Today's Scripture**
   1 Timothy 2:5
2. **Memory Verse**
   1 Timothy 2:5
   There is only one God. And there is only one way that people can reach God. That way is through Jesus Christ, who is also a man.
3. **Reference Scripture**
   Luke 2:52
   Hebrews 2:14
4. **Objectives**
   a. Let us know clearly that Jesus Christ is truly God and yet He came to the world as a human man.
   b. Let us be enlightened that because Jesus Himself was a man, He understands our human weaknesses and can help us. So let us always draw nearer to Jesus.

LEADING QUESTIONS

> ### What did the Apostle Paul say of Jesus Christ?
> (1 Timothy 2:5)

> ### Why did Jesus have to come in the flesh and be like us?
> (Hebrews 2:14)

TODAY'S MESSAGE

Jesus Christ both is God and was man. In the previous lesson we learned He is truly God. Now we will study that He was truly man and also the purpose of His becoming man.

Biblical Proofs That He was Truly Man

The gospel of John, which clearly teaches about His deity, also gives a very detailed account of Jesus' humanity. The Apostle John first called Jesus Christ, "Logos" (the Word) and this "Logos" is God (John1:1-2).

149

Then he said:

The Word became a man and lived among us. (John 1:14)

This means that God-clothed human flesh dwelt among us. Now let us study some scriptures concerning the human character of Jesus Christ.

First, Jesus Christ was born and grew in the flesh in just the same way as you and I were born and grew up. Luke described Jesus' childhood:

Jesus continued to learn more and more and to grow physically. People liked him and he pleased God.

From this verse (Luke 2:52) we can see Jesus grew in four aspects:

1. He grew in knowledge – *Jesus continued to learn more and more* ....
2. He grew physically – *.... and to grow physically*
3. He grew spiritually – *.... he pleased God.*
4. He grew socially – *People liked him* ......

Jesus Christ developed in every area of life as other human beings develop.

Second, Jesus Christ was the same as man in that He ate, drank, slept, became angry and loved. He had the same emotions and feelings as we have. Jesus felt hungry as we do (Luke 24:41) so He ate. He was tired so He fell asleep (Luke 8:23). He agonized (John 11:33, 38), rejoiced (John 15:11), loved (John 13:34, 14:21, 11:11) and cried (John 11:35).

Third, Jesus Christ Himself witnessed that He was truly man. Jesus let people know He was truly God and also did not deny that He was truly man. Jesus witnessed that He was man (Matthew 4:4, Luke 4:4) and He made no excuse when He was accused of His human attributes (Matthew 11:19, Luke 7:34). Jesus also made sure that He had, like all other human beings, a body (Matthew 26:12, 26; Mark 14:8, 22; Luke 22:19) and other physical members such as hands and feet (Luke 24:39).

Fourth, Jesus had all of the elements of humanity as we do but one thing was different – there was no sin in Jesus.

Although Jesus too felt distress over the death He would soon be confronted with (Luke 12:50), and expressed His pain by crying out loudly on the cross, (Matthew 27:46, Mark 15:34) He knew no sin.

Jesus Christ also recognized the evil which surrounded Him but He never succumbed to the evil. Even Pilate who indeed hung Jesus on the cross confessed three times:

150

"I can find nothing to charge against this man." (John 18:38, 19:4,6)

The writer of Hebrews also told:

> *For our high priest is able to understand our weaknesses. When he lived on earth, he was tempted in every way that we are, but he did not sin.* (Hebrews 4:15)

Jesus Christ Himself asked:

> *Can any of you prove that I am guilty of sin? If I am telling the truth, why don't you believe me?* (John 8:46)

The Purpose of Jesus Becoming Man

Jesus Christ was above all creatures and above all the angels. Then why did this glorious Jesus have to come to the earth in the form of humanity?

The first purpose of Jesus' coming as a man was to save sinful man by taking upon Himself man's sins, sickness, sorrows and death.

Hebrew 2:14-15 states the purpose of Jesus' coming, clothed in the garment of humanity, as:

> *These children are people with physical bodies. So Jesus himself became like them and had the same experiences they have. He did this so that, by dying, he could destroy the one who has the power of death. That one is the devil. Jesus became like men and died so that he could free them. They were like slaves all their lives because of their fear of death.*

Because the Son of God is made "after the power of an endless life" he cannot die. Therefore in order for Jesus to die, He must take a different nature than His own so that He can die. The writer of Hebrews records this:

> *For this reason Jesus had to be made like His brothers in every way. He became like men so that he could be their merciful and faithful high priest in service to God. Then Jesus could bring forgiveness for their sins.* (Hebrews 2:17)

The second purpose why *"the only Son"* (John 1:18) *"came to earth and became a man"* (2 John 1:7) was to have us hear, see with our eyes, look upon, and touch *"something that has always existed"* (1 John 1:1). Though no man has ever seen God before, through the body of Jesus Christ, man became able to experience God, meet Him and touch Him. Therefore Jesus' coming in the flesh of man was the most mysterious and wondrous miracle in human history.

In conclusion, Jesus is truly God and was truly man. Though Jesus had these two natures within Him when He walked on the earth, yet

He was one person and there is no division in Him. We should have died because of our sin but Jesus came to this earth in our form to receive our punishment and to quicken us. Through His death and resurrection, we obtained eternal life and we became children of God.

CLOSING QUESTIONS

> ### In Jesus' humanity, there is one distinct difference in His nature from ours. What is it?
> (Hebrews 4:15)

> ### Name the two purposes of Jesus' coming in the flesh.
> 1. Hebrews 2:17
> 2. 1 John 1:2

> ### What is Jesus' method of atoning for our sins?
> (Hebrews 2:9)

APPLICATION

1. Jesus in the form of man was also a true model for obedience and humility. Let us reflect on ourselves – is our faith life really growing steadily in obedience and humility?

2. Let us meditate on Jesus' prayer at Gethsemane and His suffering for us. Thanks be to our Heavenly Father!

JESUS'
THREE OFFICES

1. **Today's Scripture**
   Hebrews 4:14-16
2. **Memory Verse**
   Hebrews 4:14
   > *We have a great high priest who has gone into heaven. He is Jesus the Son of God. So let us hold on to the faith we have.*
3. **Reference Scripture**
   Deuteronomy 18:15
   Revelation 17:14
4. **Objectives**
   a. By studying the three offices of Jesus Christ, we will know clearly who is the Jesus Christ that we believe in!
   b. As disciples of Jesus Christ, let us make our very best efforts to live in the likeness of Jesus: the life of a prophet, priest and king.

LEADING QUESTIONS

> **In John 4:19 how was Jesus Christ described?**

> **How does Hebrews 4:14 describe Jesus?**

> **How did the Apostle John see Jesus in Revelation 17:14 and what does that particular capacity mean?**

TODAY'S MESSAGE

In the Bible, the office of Jesus Christ is generally divided into three areas, the offices of prophet, priest and king. Most of the Old Testament messages relate to these three areas of ministry. God proclaimed His message to His people many times and in many ways through His inspired prophets, and it was finally consummated and expanded in Jesus Christ (Hebrews 1:1).

Today we will study these three offices that Jesus completed and expanded.

The Office of Prophet

The duty of a prophet covered the widest scope of all the ministry of Jesus. His prophetic work was planned by God a long time ago (Isaiah 61:1-2). So when Jesus came to this world, He fulfilled His duty as God had preordained. Jesus revealed God better than any other prophet (Matthew 11:27, John 16:15). His teachings were with an authority and power that were different from the teachers of the law (Matthew 7:28-29, Mark 1:22), and His proclamation differed from other men (John 3:34). All these are the necessary elements in carrying out Jesus' prophetic office. Then what were the particular characteristics of His ministry as a prophet?

First, His way of teaching was unique. He used many parables to enable people easily to understand the secrets of the heavenly kingdom. His messages touched the listeners deeply and they were moved under His grace (Matthew 7:29, John 1:14). Indeed the work of prophet was perfected in Christ.

Second, a special relationship between the work of the prophet and the Holy Spirit should be noted. The prophetic duty of Jesus Christ began through the Holy Spirit, blossomed through the Holy Spirit, and was consummated through the Holy Spirit. After His ascension, His spirit, that is the Holy Spirit, succeeded Jesus' prophetic ministry.

The Office of Priest

The priesthood of Christ is based upon the priesthood of Israel that developed throughout their history. The duty of the priests in Judaism included a duty of mediating between man and God. The priest represents his people and comes forward to God on behalf of the people. So Jesus filled an intermediary role to offer sacrifices to God for mankind. And He blesses His people through the confirmation of God's acceptance of Jesus' sacrifice.

As we saw through the sacrifice offering rituals in the Old Testament, we can find Jesus as priest in His ministry of giving Himself as the sin offering of mankind to God (Hebrews 2:17). Jesus Christ indeed became the High Priest for us.

Jesus Christ became our High Priest before God. An offerer's hand on the sacrifice animal signified the transfer of the offerer's sin to that animal as it was being offered to God. It was a "model" that was to be fulfilled by Jesus when He bore all man's sins and died on the cross (Leviticus 3:2, 8,13; Isaiah 53:6; 2 Corinthians 5:21). Now, through the shed blood of Jesus, we are free to enter the Most Holy Place (Hebrews 10:19), because Jesus Christ, by giving Himself to God, broke down the wall between God and us (Ephesians 2:14).

Truly, Jesus is our only mediator (1 Timothy 2:5).
He is there now before God to help us. (Hebrews 9:24)

The Office of King

Jesus' ministry also includes the office of king in addition to the offices of prophet and priest. Two points in Jesus' kingship should be noted; its legitimacy and its character.

The legitimacy of Jesus' kingship
a. His birth: Jesus Christ was born as a king. He came from "the family of David" (Luke 2:4). Seeing His birth, the angels sang that He would become king. Even the Pharisees acknowledged the Christ as a descendant of David (Matthew 22:41, Mark 12:35, Luke 20:41).

The Apostle Paul also said:
....Jesus Christ our Lord. As a man, he was born from the family of David. (Romans 1:3)
From the human point of view, Jesus was king as He came from King David's family, and from the divine point of view, He is the Son of God.

b. His appointing: David's becoming king was totally because of God's choosing and anointing. In the same way, Jesus became "King of kings" (Revelation 17:14) because God anointed Him. The Apostle Paul wrote:
So God raised Christ to the highest place. God made the name of Christ greater than every other name. (Philippians 2:9)
And Luke told of Peter proclaiming:
"So, all the people of Israel should know this truly: God has made Jesus both Lord and Christ. He is the man you nailed to the cross!" (Acts 2:36)
Jesus was a God-appointed king.

c. His rule: A king's duty is to rule over the people. This duty was completely fulfilled by Jesus. By His boundless power and love Jesus conquered men's hearts and won them. Therefore Jesus sufficiently qualifies as "King of kings".

The nature of Jesus' kingship
First, His kingship was not of this world, but of the kingdom of

heaven. Jesus Himself proclaimed:
> "My kingdom does not belong to this world." (John 18:36)

And His kingship was universal as we read in Matthew 8:11:
> "Many people will come from the east and from the west. They will sit and eat with Abraham, Isaac and Jacob in the kingdom of heaven."

Also the great commission in Matthew 28:19 witnesses to the universality of Jesus' kingship:
> "So go and make followers of all people in the world. Baptize them in the name of the Father and the Son and the Holy Spirit."

The three offices of Christ are:
- prophet, to reveal God to people
- priest, to mediate between God and mankind and offer sacrifice to God
- king, to rule.

All these offices of Jesus Christ unite harmoniously towards one goal, the salvation of mankind.

CLOSING QUESTIONS

> ### What are the two characteristics of Jesus' ministry in carrying out His prophetic duty?
> (Find the answer from today's message.)

> ### What resulted from Jesus fulfilling His ministry as priest?
> (Hebrews 9:25-26; 10:19)

> ### What are the two special characteristics of Jesus' kingship?
> (Find the answer from today's message.)

APPLICATION

1. Meditate on the priesthood of Jesus. How does it relate to you and me personally?

2. Discuss with each other Jesus' ministry as king.

JESUS'
CHARACTER

1. **Today's Scripture**
   Matthew 11:27-30
2. **Memory Verse**
   1 John 2:6
   Whoever says that God lives in him must live as Jesus lived.
3. **Reference Scripture**
   Acts 3:14
   2 Corinthians 8:9
4. **Objectives**
   a. Let us study the character of Jesus Christ.
   b. Let us ponder how we can follow and develop the character of Jesus in ourselves.

LEADING QUESTIONS

If God lives in us, how should we live?
(1 John 2:6)

How was Jesus depicted in Acts: 3:14?

The Apostle Paul writes "Christ was rich, but .... he became poor."
Why did he become poor?
(2 Corinthians 8:9)

TODAY'S MESSAGE

One of the many purposes of Jesus' incarnation is to give us a standard to follow. If we want to discover real Christian living standards or Christian ideals, it is very important to study Jesus' character. What, then, are the major characteristics of Jesus?

Jesus' Holiness

By nature, Jesus is holy and without sin (Hebrews 4:15). He was also sinless in His actions, *"not influenced by sinners"* (Hebrews 7:26), and always did things pleasing to His Father (John 8:29).

Therefore, when we look upon this Holy Jesus, we cannot but cry out like Isaiah:

> *"Oh no! I will be destroyed. I am not pure. And I live among people who are not pure. But I have seen the King, the Lord of heaven's armies."* (Isaiah 6:5)

Or like Peter:

> *"Go away from me, Lord. I am a sinful man!"* (Luke 5:9)

As Jesus is holy, we must be holy (1 Peter 1:16). Though we are powerless and impure, we, under the guidance of the Holy Spirit, need to set our hearts to try to imitate the examples that Jesus has shown to us. When we make this effort, our Lord Jesus will bless us:

> *Those who go to him for help are happy. They are never disgraced.* (Psalm 34:5)

Jesus' Love

The love that Jesus loves us with is such a pure love that we can never explain it by the love with which we love Jesus. Then what are the qualities of Jesus' love?

First, His love is the love that flows from His Father (John 14:21).

Second, what He said was all from the Word of God. Jesus loved the Father's Word the most. When tempted, He quoted scriptures beginning with, *"It is written..."* and He also taught the verses revealing Himself to the people (Luke 4:16-21, 24:44-45). He also declared that the Word of God is always true (John 10:34-36).

Third, Jesus' love is one that is always flowing out towards human beings. He loved everyone regardless of status, wealthy or poor, high or low, male or female, child or adult, and no matter how far they wandered into sin. He was accused of being *"a friend of tax collectors and sinners"* (Matthew 11:19). Jesus loved us so much that He finally poured out His own life to save us (John 10:11, 15:13; Romans 5:8).

Lastly, His love is the love that even loves His enemies. He taught disciples, *"love your enemies"* (Matthew 5:44). Jesus Himself prayed for the people who put Him on the cross (Luke 23:34). When we were still enemies Jesus extended His loving arm to us (Romans 5:10).

Jesus' Humility

His humility was well manifested in His earthly ministry. Jesus is truly the wealthiest One, Who owns all the glory of the heavens, but for our sake He chose to be poor. In order to relate to the people better, He took our poverty on Himself (2 Corinthians 8:9). As a new-born baby He was laid in a manger, not even in a proper room – this is the best example of His becoming poor (Luke 2:7). He did not own a tomb and had to be buried in a borrowed tomb (Matthew 27:57-60). Jesus also did the most humble thing of all – washing His disciples' feet Himself (John 13:14).

Jesus said Himself:
"In the same way, the Son of Man did not come to be served. He came to serve." (Mark 10:45)

Jesus' Meekness

Christ Himself said, *"I am gentle and humble in spirit"*. (Matthew 11:29). His meekness is described in Matthew 12:20 quoting Isaiah:
He will not break a crushed blade of grass. He will not put out even a weak flame. He will continue until he makes fair judgement win the victory.

Christ lived in total meekness. He treated meekly both the repentant sinners (Luke 7:37-50), and Peter who once denied Him (John 21:15-23). From the way in which he treated the traitor Judas, and the people who hung Him on the cross, Jesus' meek character stands out even more (Matthew 26:50, John 13:21). Truly He was meek and did *"not argue or shout. No one will hear his voice in the streets."* (Matthew 12:19)

Jesus' Obedience

The obedience of Jesus Christ was a complete obedience in all aspects.

First, He obeyed His physical parents (Luke 2:51).

Second, He obeyed God by keeping all the moral laws. He *"did not sin"* (Hebrews 4:15) and *"had no sin"* (2 Corinthians 5:21).
He is holy; he has no sin in him. He is pure and not influenced by sinners. (Hebrews 7:26)

To God, Jesus' sinlessness satisfies God's perfect righteousness and to man, Jesus' sinlessness gave no ground to find fault with (John 8:46). To prevent people's misunderstanding He even obeyed to the point of paying tax to a human government (Matthew 17:24-27).

Third, He obeyed until He died (Philippians 2:8) to save us.

> ... *one man obeyed God, and many will be made right.* (Romans 5:19)

Also Peter described Jesus' obedience:

> *Christ Himself died for you. And that one death paid for your sins. He was not guilty but he died for those that are guilty. He did this to bring you all to God. His body was killed but he was made alive in the spirit.* (1 Peter 3:18)

Jesus' constant obedience throughout His life made it possible for Him to be the "lamb without blemish and without spot." Thus only Jesus could be our subsititutionary sacrifice.

Jesus' Prayer Life

We read:

> *While Jesus lived here on earth, he prayed to God and asked God for help. He prayed with loud cries and tears to the One who could save him from death. And his prayer was heard because he left it all up to God.* (Hebrews 5:7)

God does not need to pray, yet Jesus, who is very God, prayed and this attitude represents His humility so well. Also, He prayed often. Sometimes He prayed in the presence of His disciples but mostly He prayed alone. He spent long hours in His prayer and at times prayed all through the night (Matthew 14:23, Luke 6:12). Prior to His important ministry, He always prepared with prayer. Before His ministry in Galilee (Mark 1:35-38), before He chose the twelve disciples, and at the Garden of Gethsemane He prayed with all His might.

The characteristics of Jesus we have learned today are the very characteristics we should develop and follow in our daily walk with Jesus. When these characteristics dwell in us, we will become mature in the Lord Jesus, and these characteristics will cause the fruit of the Holy Spirit to abound in us and bring much glory to our Heavenly Father.

CLOSING QUESTIONS

> ### Name the four characteristics of Christ's love.
> (Find the answer from today's message.)

> ### Share with each other how Jesus obeyed
> ### in three points.
> (Find answer from today's message.)

> ### Name the points of the model we should follow
> ### in Jesus' prayer in each of the following verses:
> ### a. Matthew 26:44
> ### b. Luke 22:44
> ### c. John 11:41-42

APPLICATION

1. Today we reviewed six points of Jesus' character. Ask yourself which ones you lack and pray to the Lord to change you to be like Him.

2. Think deeply about each of the characteristics of Jesus we have studied today and see how they relate to our daily living. Let us practise them one by one.

JESUS'
EXALTATION

1. **Today's Scripture**
   Philippians 2:5-11
2. **Memory Verse**
   Philippians 2:10
   God wants every knee to bow to Jesus – everyone in heaven, on earth and under the earth.
3. **Reference Scripture**
   Ephesians 1:19-23
   1 Peter 3:21-22
4. **Objectives**
   a. How did Jesus become *"highly exalted"* (Philippians 2:9, AV)? Let us study how He became so honoured.
   b. What is the meaning and purpose of Christ's exaltation? How does this relate to us?

LEADING QUESTIONS

> ### What is the reason that God raised Jesus Christ to the highest place?
> (Philippians 2:8-9; note the word "so")

> ### Where is Jesus Christ now?
> (1 Peter 3:22)

> ### Whom does He rule over?
> (1 Peter 3:22)

TODAY'S MESSAGE

*T*hat power is the same as the great strength God used to raise Christ from death and put him at his right side in heaven. God made Christ more important than all rulers, authorities, powers and kings. Christ is more important than anything in this world or in the next world. God put everything under his power. And God made him the head over everything for the church. (Ephesians 1:20-22)

In this scripture, Paul expresses well four aspects of Jesus' exaltation: His resurrection, His ascension, His sitting at the right side of God, and lastly, His return as the Head of all. In other words, the content of His exaltation tells how God awarded blessing and glory to Jesus after He had completed all His lowly life and suffering on earth. Now let us go over the meanings of these aspects of Jesus' exaltation.

Christ's Resurrection

If the nailing on the cross was the peak of Christ's suffering, His resurrection was the first gateway to His glory. Because of all the glory due Him, His ascension, sitting at the right hand of God, and return as the Head, all began from His resurrection. Therefore, though His resurrection is meaningful as a historical fact, it has deeper significance in terms of His receipt of glory. Accordingly, in this section we will focus His resurrection in the context of His glory, instead of in the historical fact of His resurrection. Then what is the meaning of Jesus' resurrection in the light of His exaltation?

First, His resurrection proclaimed that the power of God is far above the power of death (Ephesians 1:20-21).

Second, His resurrection became the sign that He is truly the Son of God (Romans 1:4).

Third, His resurrection witnessed to God's acceptance of Jesus and the work of Jesus.

Fourth, His resurrection was the completion of God's plan for the redemption of man (John 19:30).

Fifth, His resurrection is proof of eternal life. It is also the prelude to the new resurrected life which the dead in Christ will know on the resurrection day, the life that no death can overcome (Revelation 1:18).

Lastly, His resurrection means the Son of God's triumphal entry into the new kingdom, the kingdom of glory. Then an interesting question immediately arises, what was the resurrected body of Jesus like?

His body was perfectly recognizable to human eyes (Luke 24:39-40; John 20:24-29). His resurrected body was the same as the natural body so He ate food (Luke 24:43), yet His body was a transformed body that surpassed the limit of time and place (John 20:26). God

164

punished Jesus' body on the cross as the body for all sinners, and through the resurrection God transformed Jesus' body into a glorified body.

Christ's Ascension

According to the Bible, Christ's ascension was a visible instance to the human eyes (Mark 16:19; Luke 24:50-51; Acts 1:9-11). His ascension is directly linked to His saying in John 14:2 to the disciples:

> *"There are many rooms in my Father's house. I would not tell you this if it were not true."*

So Jesus' ascension meant He was departing to prepare a place for His people and He will return for them again (John 14:3). Also, His actual departure from the earth has fulfilled the condition of the Holy Spirit's coming:

> *"But I tell you the truth. It is better for you that I go away. When I go away I will send the Helper to you. If I do not go away, then the Helper will not come."* (John 16:7)

The gift of salvation was given to be preached to all mankind, not only to Judea but unto the ends of the earth.

Christ's Seat at God's Right Side

"The right side of God" is often mentioned in the Bible – Acts 7:55-56; Romans 8:34; Ephesians 1:20; Hebrews 1:3, 10:12, 12:2; 1 Peter 3:22. This phrase is mostly used to signify the union of Jesus and God in glory and power. Then what is the original purpose and meaning of: *"he . . . sat down at the right side of God, the Great One in heaven"* (Hebrews 1:3)?

First, His sitting at the right side of God means God has *"put all things under his control"* (1 Corinthians 15:27; Hebrews 2:8). Also, He is governing all the world:

> *"All power in heaven and on earth is given to me."* (Matthew 28:18)

Jesus is the King of kings.

The second purpose of Jesus' sitting at the right side of God is to continue His work of mediator between God and man, and the work of salvation.

Christ's Return

Christ's exaltation will be fulfilled by His return. At that time, His ministry of redemption will end and He will return to judge the world. And God's eternal kingdom will be established. Jesus' return will be the peak of His exaltation. For this moment He was resurrected and ascended into Heaven and has been sitting at the right side of God. Now let us study how He will return and what it will be like.

First, His return will actually take place. His return will be visible to human eyes. The scripture says no one but the Father knows the date and time when He will come (Acts 1:7). But He is to come (Acts 1:11; 2 Thessalonians 1:10; Revelation 1:7). That is why we should not be slothful, but be diligent every day in preparing to meet Him as if He were to return today.

The second purpose of Jesus' return is judgement. Jesus Himself declared that the Father had given the Son power to judge (John 5:22, 9:39). The Apostle Paul also said:
> We shall all stand before the judgement seat of Christ. (Romans 14:10 AV)

On that day, the absolute sovereign ruler, Jesus Christ, will judge all. But His judgement will be just and perfect with wisdom and love.

In conclusion Jesus became obedient to God unto death on the cross. God highly exalted Him and made Him the King of kings, Sovereign judge, and Head of all the nations. The exaltation of Christ is the result of His humility and lowliness. Though He is still highly exalted, yet He is still praying unceasingly for us, that our faith will not fail.

To complete God's redemptive work, Jesus is even today taking care of us. Not only that, but He is preparing a place for us where we will share in His glory. This work will continue until Jesus returns to earth again.

CLOSING QUESTIONS

What are the purposes of Jesus' ascension?
(Name two from today's message.)

What are the two purposes of Jesus sitting at the right side of God?
(Find the answer from today's message.)

How will Jesus return and what will He do?
(Acts 1:11; Romans 14:10)

APPLICATION

1. With the return of Jesus near, ask yourself, "How do I faithfully prepare for it and how should I change my ways before God to be ready?"

2. Share with each other any special blessing that you received from today's message.

THE MINISTRY OF
JESUS CHRIST

PART ONE

During His short period of three and a half years' ministry, Jesus did many more things than any other living person. The Bible declares that if all the things Jesus did were written down, even the whole world itself could not hold the books that would be written.

Before embarking on public life, Jesus was baptized in water by John the Baptist and through the Holy Spirit He was confirmed to be the Son of God. This is proof that all the works of Jesus are from God and by God's will. After forty days of fasting in the wilderness, Jesus was tempted, but He drove Satan off by quoting the Word of God. From that time on His powerful ministry began, and the short life of Jesus is summed up in His birth, suffering, death, resurrection and ascension. The ministry of Jesus consists mainly of preaching the good news of the Heavenly Kingdom, healing the sick and destroying the works of the devil. In Units Five and Six, we will study the ministry of Jesus.

The Ministry of Jesus Christ – Part One

30. Jesus is Baptized
31. Jesus is Tempted
32. Jesus Preaches the Good News of the Heavenly Kingdom
33. Jesus Calls His Disciples
34. Jesus Performs Miracles
35. Jesus Cleanses the Temple
36. Jesus Works on the Sabbath
37. Jesus Prays
38. Jesus Conquers Death
39. Jesus Bears Our Sickness
40. Jesus Casts Out Devils

JESUS IS
BAPTIZED

1. Today's Scripture
Matthew 3:13-17

2. Memory Verse
Matthew 3:16
> *Jesus was baptized and came up out of the water. Then heaven opened, and he saw God's spirit coming down on him like a dove.*

3. Reference Scripture
Romans 6:1-5

4. Objectives
  a. Through the baptized Jesus, let us learn the meaning and importance of baptism.
  b. Even the Son of God, Jesus, was baptized, as we sinners must be. Let us learn about the lowliness of Jesus.

LEADING QUESTIONS

> ### By whom was Jesus baptized?
> (Matthew 3:13)

> ### With whom was Jesus baptized?
> (Luke 3:21)

> ### What was Jesus doing when heaven opened and the Holy Spirit came down?
> (Luke 3:21)

TODAY'S MESSAGE

John the Baptist was preaching that people should change their hearts and lives because the kingdom of heaven was coming soon, and also baptizing people in the Jordan river. After thirty years of private life in Galilee, Jesus came out to the Jordan River in order to be baptized. Seeing Jesus ready to be baptized by him, John declined hurriedly:

> *"Why do you come to me to be baptized? I should be baptized by you!"*

But Jesus said:

> *"Let it be this way for now. We should do all things that are right."* (Matthew 3:15)

and offered Himself to be baptized by John.

When Jesus was baptized as well as other people, while he prayed, heaven opened and the Holy Spirit came down on Him like a dove (Luke 3:21). Through Jesus' baptism, we may learn a few lessons that God is teaching us here.

Jesus' Baptism as Preparation for Public Life

Just prior to His public life, Jesus received water baptism by John. Of course, Jesus Christ knew no sin, nor had He committed any sin. He was without blemish, yet He received the water baptism of repentance just as we sinners do, so that He could redeem man from sin. This is the love that God loves us with. Jesus' baptism teaches that we, too, at the time of conversion, should be baptized as a sign to the world of our true repentance and our willingness to bear the fruit of repentance. Going down into water means complete burial of our old person and sin, and coming up from the water symbolizes a newness of life like the resurrection, which is also a proclamation that we are born again and a new person. The Apostle Paul teaches this in Romans 6:3-4:

> *Did you forget that all of us became part of Christ when we were baptized? We shared his death in our baptism. So when we were baptized, we were buried with Christ and shared his death. We were buried with him so that we could live a new life, just as Christ was raised from death by the wonderful power of the Father.*

Let us remember that even Jesus was baptized like an ordinary sinner who had been redeemed, like us. Then how much more should *we* repent of our sins? Let us crucify our old person's greediness and lust on the cross and live a new life, the resurrected life. Let us have this experience of our faith.

Jesus Prayed

Jesus prayed when baptized. Luke 3:21 records this. John's baptism was the baptism of repentance of sin (Matthew 3:1-12). Jesus did not need to pray for repentance of sin before he was baptized, because He had never committed any sin nor knew sin (Hebrews 4:15, 1 John 3:5). Nevertheless Jesus prayed at baptism and showed us a true example.

Jesus cast out the devil through fasting and prayer. He often prayed overnight and also prayed in the mountains (Luke 6:12). Before choosing disciples he prayed (Luke 6:13). He prayed alone and also with His disciples (Luke 5:16, 9:18, 28).

Before He died on the cross for our salvation, to become our sin offering, He prayed until the sweat dripped off him like blood in the garden of Gethsemane (Luke 22:44). The Bible shows us the whole life of Jesus was a life of prayer.

In like manner, we should always pray (Luke 2:37, 18:1; 1 Thessalonians 5:17). We should pray in the Holy Spirit Who always helps us (Ephesians 6:18), and especially we should be watchful and serious lest we fall into temptation and fail in our faith (1 Peter 4:7). As long as we live we are to pray to God (Psalm 116:2).

The Son of God, Who did not even know sin, received the baptism of repentance from John the Baptist. This fact shows that Jesus Who came to earth with human life (Romans 8:3), had made Himself ready to serve before He made us ready (John 17:19). When Jesus was baptized and came up from the water, heaven opened and the Holy Spirit came down like a dove upon Jesus and the voice of God was heard:

"This is My Son and I love him. I am very pleased with him."

Here we find a very significant thing, that Jesus received baptism before He began His public life, and when He was baptized the work of the Trinity of God was clearly manifested – the Holy Spirit came down upon Jesus and God Himself witnessed that Jesus is one of the Trinity of God and the Son of God.

Just as heaven opened and the Holy Spirit came down upon Jesus when He was baptized and prayed, we believers shall also receive answers to prayer from our Heavenly Father.

Jesus' Humility

From the scene of His baptism we see Jesus' humility. He is the King of kings, the Creator of all, and the Son of God, yet He lowered Himself to be baptized by a man.

As Jesus humbled Himself like this and was baptized together with these shallow and ignorant people, God, His Father, raised Him up in an amazing way and confirmed:

"This is my Son and I love him. I am very pleased with him."

Jesus too said of Himself:
> *"I am gentle and humble in spirit."* (Matthew 11:29)

Therefore, we, as Jesus' own people, should also bear a resemblance to Jesus' humility. Humbleness is lowliness of mind, in which each one esteems others better than themselves. And to those who have this lowly attitude, wisdom (Proverbs 11:2), honour (Proverb 29:23) and joy (Isaiah 29:19) come and they can experience wondrous miracles of having God hear all their desires.

Through Jesus being baptized, we have learned three lessons:
1. Before we believers begin any work, we must search our hearts for Him to reveal sin.
2. We must follow the steps of Jesus in His prayer life.
3. We must have the mind of Jesus, the lowliest mind, one of humility.

Then, we will also live a life of miracles that experiences God's answers to our prayer, as happened when Jesus was baptized.

CLOSING QUESTIONS

What was heard from heaven when Jesus was baptized?
(Matthew 3:17)

Why did John agree to baptize Jesus?
(Matthew 3:15)

Who did we become part of when we were baptized?
(Romans 6:3)

Now consider the application of this lesson which you will find on the next page.

APPLICATION

1. Since Jesus as the Son of God was without sin, and as the Son of God He did not need to be baptized by John, yet to redeem our sins He received water baptism, are you truly overwhelmed by this love of Jesus and do you give Him due thanks?

2. Let us pray always, like our Lord Jesus did.

3. Let us be truly humble as one who is in the Lord Jesus.

JESUS IS
TEMPTED

1. **Today's Scripture**
   Matthew 4:1-11
2. **Memory Verse**
   Matthew 4:10
   > *Jesus said to the devil, "Go away from me, Satan! It is written in the Scriptures, 'You must worship the Lord your God. Serve only him!'"*
3. **Reference Scripture**
   Genesis 3:6
   Hebrews 4:15
4. **Objectives**
   a. Let us learn how Jesus became the sinners' Saviour by resisting Satan's temptation (1 Corinthians 15:45).
   b. Let us be convinced that Jesus always helps our weakness and leads us to victory.
   c. Let us also lead a Word-centred life as Jesus did.

LEADING QUESTIONS

> ### What was Jesus' physical condition like when He was tempted?
> (Matthew 4:2)

> ### Write the three temptations Jesus confronted.
> (Matthew 4:3, 6, 9)
>
> a. _____
> b. _____
> c. _____

> ### How did Jesus repel Satan's temptations?
> (Matthew 4:4,7,10)

TODAY'S MESSAGE

Baptized by John at the Jordan River, Jesus was immediately led by the Holy Spirit to the wilderness. After He had fasted there for forty days, He was tempted three times by Satan but by the Word of God, Jesus repelled all three temptations. Through the lesson of Jesus' triumph over temptation, today we will study God's love towards us and learn God's profound providence for delivering us from Satan's snares and temptations.

Why was Jesus Tempted?

Immediately after Jesus was baptized by John the Baptist, He was led by the Holy Spirit to the wilderness. Tempted by Satan after forty days of fasting, Jesus proved that He was a man in no way different from Adam. This was the first reason why Jesus was tempted by the devil.

Second, Jesus was tempted for the test of obedience to God. The first man Adam could not overcome temptation and eventually ate the fruit of knowledge of good and evil. In other words, Adam trampled down God's authority and disobeyed. Now, to Jesus the same temptation came again. In one word this temptation was a "cross-roads" with a choice of ways to follow – acknowledge God's sovereign right and just obey Him, or turn to other ways.

In His period of testing, Jesus overcame the temptation and obeyed God until He died on the cross.

The Three Temptations of Jesus

There are two kinds of temptation mentioned in the word of God. One reads "dokimazo" in Greek. This testing is given by God as a stepping stone to receive the greater blessings that God loves to bestow upon His children. God allows us to go through these kinds of testings and trials so that each one of us might be proven, and thereby be recognized as a qualified saint by withstanding these difficulties and being victorious in our faith in Christ.

Another kind of testing is called "peirazo" in Greek. This is a Satan-given temptation that brings ordeal, suffering and afflictions with intent to kill, destroy and rob us. Satan never gives us the "dokimazo" testing that upgrades us in our faith. Satan only leads us to stumble by the ensnaring trap of our sins.

Satan knows that once we succumb and fall to his temptation, we will surely receive God's judgement. We can see for ourselves God could never use us in certain places, because we would constantly give in to the temptations which are out to destroy us unless we live close to God. That is why the devil like a roaring lion is looking for someone to eat (1 Peter 5:8).

The devil tempted Adam and Eve with this "peirazo" temptation. Our first parents failed because they succumbed to this temptation of wanting things to please their sinful selves, wanting the sinful things they saw and being too proud of what they had (1 John 2:16), and were therefore cast out by God. Now the devil extended to Jesus the same temptation of "peirazo". But Jesus did not succumb to the devil's enticement.

The devil, too, knew how hungry Jesus was after the forty days' fasting, so he tempted Jesus to fill His empty stomach first by making bread out of stone. The devil used the "lust of the flesh" (1 John 2:16 in the AV) as the test object. Eve failed here, and ate the fruit of the tree of knowledge of good and evil that was pleasing to her "lust of the flesh". But Jesus' supreme concern was obedience to God's Word. This was greater than the "lust of the flesh" and Jesus proved it by saying:

> "It is written in the Scriptures, 'A person does not live only by eating bread. But a person lives by everything the Lord says.'"

After the first test, the devil, even quoting scripture verses from Psalm 91:11-12, again tempted Jesus to jump down from the pinnacle of the temple in order to put God to the test, and also to show off in front of the Jewish people that He is truly the Son of God. Eve, too, at the garden of Eden was ensnared by this "lust of the eyes" (wanting the sinful things she saw) and fell by taking the fruit of knowledge of good and evil. Needless to say, Jesus could have jumped unharmed. He need not have sprained so much as a toe, even if He had jumped from the pinnacle of the temple to the farthest depths of the Kidron valley. If Jesus had jumped down like that at the time of the evening sacrifice, it would have been a great spectacle for the crowd who would probably have followed Jesus immediately as their great leader.

But Jesus subdued the "lust of the eyes" and resisted the devil by speaking the Word of God:

> "It also says in the Scriptures, 'Do not test the Lord your God.'"

Lastly the tempter took Jesus to a high mountain, showed Him all the glory of the world kingdoms and offered to give all of them to Jesus if He would worship him. It could have been one way for Jesus to take back the world and mankind that were legally handed over to Satan by Adam's fall. Jesus came to the world with that purpose anyhow. But He knew only too well that if He accepted the way Satan offered, it would only bring destruction. Jesus did not choose or act on His own to take such an easy and comfortable way to solve the problems of mankind, but He chose the death on the cross, God's very own provision. Jesus Christ revealed His absolute obedience to God through His confession when He proclaimed:

"It is written in the Scriptures, 'You must worship the Lord your God. Serve only him.' "

But Eve, who pursued her "pride of life" (1 John 2:16 in the AV), dared to become wise like God, and fell.

Jesus broke all the "peirazo" temptations of Satan and therefore became the sacrifice offering for our sins though His total obedience to God.

When We Are Tempted

What are the lessons we are learning from the temptations Jesus dealt with?

First, the time Jesus was tempted by Satan was after the Holy Spirit came down upon Him like a dove, and also after a voice was heard from heaven. It is the same today. The devil tempts us at the times we are faring well. When we are being promoted, when we are praised by others, when we are beginning to live comfortably or we are getting wealthy and when we enter a deeper level of God's grace with the blessing of a fast growing faith, these are the times Satan tempts us. Satan fundamentally abhors our faith and life when all is going well. Satan tempts us when we are very much alive, just as a hunter aims his gun at a live animal, not a dead one. So the Apostle Paul admonishes us:

So anyone who thinks he is standing strong should be careful not to fall. (1 Corinthians 10:12)

Second, we notice the place where Jesus was tempted. It was in the wilderness. There is a spiritual parallel here. The meaning of wilderness indicates our present life. The people of Israel came out of Egypt but spent a transit life for forty years in the wilderness before they entered the promised land, Canaan. We, too, are delivered from the wicked world (our Egypt) when we accept Jesus Christ as our Saviour, but we also are destined to live a sojourner's life in a "wilderness", which is the world we are now living in. Later, in the future, once we enter the heavenly kingdom there will be no temptation, but while we are living in the wilderness of our present life, we have no choice but to confront storms, hunger, thirst, misunderstandings and days when the sun seems to be scorching hot. Therefore, in this wilderness of life we need to be watchful and pray always to our Father, *"Lead us not into temptation"*.

Third, when we are tempted we should discipline ourselves staunchly to obey God! We should never discard our faith, but hold fast to the truth that God is a good God and He will save us. Regardless of the circumstances that befall us, we should resolutely determine to obey God. Also we should resist temptation by the Word of God as Jesus did, beginning with "*It is written .....*". Without making such a firm resolution in our hearts and minds towards our absolute trust and obedience to God, we will not be able to win over the devil's temptation easily. We cannot defeat the devil just by quoting God's Word because he uses it to tempt us sometimes. Furthermore, we should always seek the help of the Holy Spirit in every temptation, because the Holy Spirit is the Comforter who was sent and he is ready to rescue us every time we are in trouble.

CLOSING QUESTIONS

> ### Who is the only one we must worship and serve?
> (Matthew 4:10)

> ### How does a temptation begin to interest us?
> (James 1:14)

> ### We are not to love the things of the world. What does the "love of the world" produce in the lives of people, that develops into temptation?
> (1 John 2:16)

APPLICATION

1. Let us strive to become absolutely obedient children of God.

2. Let us become the Holy-Spirit-filled believers who are able to resist Satan's temptation.

3. Always meditate on the Word of God, store scriptures in your heart and quote these scriptures as your weapon to repel the devil.

JESUS PREACHES
THE GOOD NEWS OF
THE HEAVENLY
KINGDOM

1. **Today's Scripture**
   Matthew 4:12-17
2. **Memory Verse**
   Matthew 4:17
   From that time Jesus began to preach saying, "Change your hearts and lives, because the kingdom of heaven is coming soon."
3. **Reference Scripture**
   Mark 1:15
   Luke 17:20-21
4. **Objectives**
   a. Let us spread the good news of God's kingdom as Jesus did.
   b. Let us always remember that when we preach the gospel, the devil will flee and the kingdom of God will expand. Let us never forget this fact.

LEADING QUESTIONS

> ### Whose prophecy was fulfilled when Jesus left Nazareth and moved to Capernaum?
> (Matthew 4:13-14)

> ### What did Jesus preach?
> (Mark 1:14)

> ### Why did Jesus say "Change your hearts and lives and believe the Good News!"
> (Mark 1:15)

TODAY'S MESSAGE

After the baptism and temptation, Jesus went to the land of Galilee. After John, who was sent beforehand to prepare the way for Jesus, had completed his job and was put into jail, Jesus began to preach the good news:

"The right time has come. The kingdom of God is near. Change your hearts and lives and believe the Good News!" (Mark 1:15)

Today we will study the substance of the good news that Jesus preached.

The Kingdom of God is Near

Jesus preached:

"The right time has come. The kingdom of God is near."

This tells us that the fullness of God's time for the redemption of mankind had come and His kingdom was near. Jesus' words, *"the kingdom of God is near"*, have a far deeper meaning than that the kingdom of God was approaching closely or that it was already present here.

As the Son of God, Jesus Himself is also God and at the very time and place where God is, the kingdom of God is there too. Therefore whenever and wherever God the Son stood, as a human being, the kingdom of God existed right there. Thus, when the Pharisees asked when the kingdom of God would come (Luke 17:20-21) Jesus replied:

"God's kingdom is coming, but not in a way that you will be able to see with your eyes. People will not say, 'Look, God's kingdom is here!' or 'There it is!' No, God's kingdom is within you."

This is because when we acknowledge Jesus, we welcome Him into our hearts and our lives to live and rule, and rely on Him. That is where the kingdom of God is.

The Pharisees slandered Jesus, saying:

"Jesus uses the power of Beelzebul to force demons out of people. Beelzebul is the ruler of demons." (Matthew 12:24)

But Jesus said in Matthew 12:28:

"But if I use the power of God's spirit to force out demons, this shows that the kingdom of God has come to you."

Furthermore, when John the Baptist sent his disciples and asked:

"Are you the man who John said was coming, or should we wait for another one?"

Jesus answered:

> *"Go back to John and tell him about the things you hear and see: The blind can see. The crippled can walk. People with harmful skin diseases are healed. The deaf can hear. The dead are raised to life. And the Good News is told to the poor."* (Matthew 11:4, 5)

John was asking whether the kingdom of God had arrived yet or not, while Jesus confirmed that the kingdom of God was *already* existing, giving signs of its presence.

Today, too, Jesus Christ is within us through the Holy Spirit, the Comforter Who is in nature the same God as Jesus Himself. Where Jesus is, the kingdom of God is. Where the kingdom of God comes, devils flee, the sick are raised, sins are forgiven, the good news is preached. These things take place all the time. And today the Church is the kingdom of God where these works of God continue to happen.

"Change Your Hearts and Lives and Believe the Good News"

The gospel in Greek is "evangelion", meaning good news. What could be the best "good news" to a human being, after all? What is it that mankind has been yearning for, generation after generation, from the bottom of his heart?

It is the news of the forgiveness of sins and the restoration of a right relationship with God again. Since Adam and Eve fell, mankind had become a "lost existence". Man lost his Creator, God. Man lost the joy of living, which was in the garden of Eden. Man lost his neighbours. Man lost his true self. People did not know where they came from, why they were living and where they were heading.

To this mankind, the good news of God arrived. That good news was and is:

> *For God loved the world so much that he gave his only Son. God gave his Son so that whoever believes in him may not be lost but have eternal life.* (John 3:16)

The good news is Jesus Christ.

Where this good news was preached, that is, wherever Jesus moved, good things happened. The blind saw. The devil-possessed were cleansed. The poor and outcast were honoured, and those isolated people like the Samaritan woman and Zacchaeus tasted the joy of life that they had never had before.

Therefore when Jesus said, *"believe the good news"* He meant, "believe Me, Jesus Christ!" He identified Himself with His good news by saying:

> *"Whoever wants to save his life will give up true life. But whoever gives up his life for me and the Good News will have true life forever."* (Mark 8:35)

In order to believe this good news and to enter the kingdom of God, repentance is essential. Repentance is "metanoia" in Greek, which means a turnabout of 180 degrees, from the past direction one was headed for, to the new direction, a new life. You should discard your old life in which you followed your will instead of following God's will. Repentance is not merely that you are sorry for your past sins, and ashamed of them. Repentance means you are turning away from your old way.

> *I forget the things that are past. I try as hard as I can to reach the goal that is before me.* (Philippians 3:13)

Once we have confessed our sins before God and sought His forgiveness, we must believe and trust God for His forgiveness.

Therefore, strictly speaking, repentance is not a past-oriented retrospect but a future-oriented prospect. Repentance enables one to look forward and advance in Christian living. Therefore repentance and faith are working together at the same moment.

Preach the Good News!

We have the awesome responsibility of preaching the good news to the world.

> *"I give you these powers freely. So help other people freely."* (Matthew 10:8)

We are called to usher our family members and neighbours into the kingdom of God. To do so we should preach the good news of Jesus Christ. We should deliver nothing but the good news, not our human knowledge or ideas. Even Jesus Christ never preached about Himself. He always witnessed about God the Father:

> *"The things I teach are not my own. My teaching comes from him who sent me."* (John 7:16)

> *"The things I taught were not from myself. The Father who sent me told me what to say and what to teach."* (John 12:49)

Therefore when we preach we should preach Jesus Christ only. As Jesus' disciples, sent by Him, we should not be ashamed of His good news. Being ashamed of the good news is being ashamed of Jesus. The Apostle Paul declared:

I am proud of the Good News. It is the power God uses to save everyone who believes .... (Romans 1:16)

We too should not be ashamed of the good news of Christ and preach it so that the power of God is revealed.

When we preach Jesus Christ, the kingdom of God comes to the people and God sovereignly rules through His supernatural power. The miracle of changes in our circumstances and those with us is always taking place!

CLOSING QUESTIONS

> ### What was in God's command to Jesus when He spoke for the Father?
> (John 12:49-50)

> ### What is the reason Paul was proud of the good news?
> (Romans 1:16)

> ### What are the two ways to enter the kingdom of God?
> (Mark 1:15)

APPLICATION

1. Ask yourself whether you are ashamed of the good news or not. The good news is the power God uses to save everyone who believes. Let us boast of this good news very boldly.

2. When we win souls, let us diligently preach the Word of God as Jesus did and Paul did. Then we will see wondrous miracles manifested in our lives.

JESUS CALLS
HIS DISCIPLES

1. **Today's Scripture**
   Luke 5:1-11
2. **Memory Verse**
   Luke 5:11
   > *When the men brought their boats to the shore, they left everything and followed Jesus.*
3. **Reference Scripture**
   Matthew 4:17-22
   John 1:35-42
4. **Objectives**
   a. Let us realize again that our Lord Jesus chose us as His disciples for the job of preaching the good news about the kingdom of God.
   b. Let us remember our Lord Jesus chooses and uses busy people as His disciples.
   c. Let us renew our resolution to follow only Jesus.

LEADING QUESTIONS

> **Though Peter had toiled all night without catching anything, what caused him to put his net in the water again?**
> (Luke 5:5)

> **After experiencing the miracle, what confession did Peter make?**
> (Luke 5:8)

> **What did Jesus say he would make of his disciples and how would it happen?**
> (Matthew 4:19)

TODAY'S MESSAGE

As soon as He started public life, Jesus did the job of electing His disciples. We can see Jesus did a really wise thing to train His disciples to take the good news about the kingdom

189

of God into the world, at a time when any communication and transport systems were not developed. Today, too, Jesus calls us to become His disciples and commits His work to us.

The Calling of His Disciples

Wherever Jesus went, huge crowds followed to listen to His words. One day on the shore of Galilee, swamped by the multitude, there was not even a place for Jesus to stand, so he got into a boat and asked to be pushed off a little from the shore, and He preached the good news about the kingdom of God from the boat.

The owner of the boat was Peter. He had cast nets all night long but caught nothing. At the time he offered his boat to Jesus he was washing his nets with an empty heart. Peter could see Jesus from the nearest seat and as he listened to what Jesus said, peace and faith stirred in his heart. Right at that moment, Jesus commanded Peter:

"Take the boat into deep water. If you will put your nets in the water you will catch some fish."

Although Peter remembered his night's experience, he simply obeyed Jesus' command.

"You say to put the nets in the water, so I will."

The scripture says Peter caught a great number of fish, enough to fill even two boats at a time. Peter immediately fell down at Jesus' knees and confessed:

"Go away from me, Lord. I am a sinful man!"

Jesus said to Peter:

"Don't be afraid. From now on you will be fishermen for men."

He called Peter, Andrew, John and James as His disciples. Jesus also called other disciples but He never used human standards to select them.

When Jesus chose His disciples, He always called busy people who were working at their jobs. If a person works hard and succeeds over one thing, he will succeed over other things in the same manner.

Therefore, when we are committed to soul-winning work, we should not excuse ourselves with: "I cannot do it because I am busy."

The Duty of the Disciples

Then what is the job of Jesus' disciples?

First, a disciple of Jesus should represent, through his own living, our good God. When Peter cast out his net into the deep water in obedience to Jesus' command, he caught a great many fish. The glory of God was manifested and the power of Jesus Christ was proven before the eyes of the watching crowd on the shore. Also, when the disciple Andrew obeyed Jesus and presented a mere five loaves of bread and two fish, another miracle of feeding a multitude took place. There were five thousand men. If women and children had been counted it would have been several tens of thousands. Likewise, a disciple of Jesus should let the power of God be manifested through his faith and obedience so that many can be led to the kingdom of God.

Second, a disciple of Jesus should be a "fisherman" catching people. For a fisherman to catch fish, he needs fishing tools, and the tools in the hands of Jesus' disciples should be the Word of God.

By the Word of God, he should comfort wounded hearts, give hope to the despairing, and supply wisdom to those in need of wisdom.
> *God's word is alive and working. It is sharper than a sword sharpened on both sides. It cuts all the way into us, where the soul and the spirit are joined. It cuts to the centre of our joints and our bones. And God's word judges the thoughts and feelings in our hearts.* (Hebrews 4:12)

By the Word of God, we should fish dying men from the sea of death.

Third, a disciple of Jesus should have the power of Jesus. Jesus gave His twelve disciples:
> *.... power to drive out evil spirits and to heal every kind of disease and sickness.* (Matthew 10:1)

Jesus also commanded His disciples:
> *"When you go, preach this: 'The kingdom of heaven is coming soon.' Heal the sick. Give dead people life again. Heal those who have harmful skin diseases. Force demons to leave people. I give you these powers freely. So help other people freely."* (Matthew 10:7-8)

Jesus' disciples are the people who do the works of Jesus. Jesus Christ came to this world and preached good news to the poor. He freed the captives of sins, gave eternal life to people blinded by the *"lust of the flesh, lust of the eyes, and the pride of life"* (1 John 2:16 AV). Jesus made them see again, and proclaimed a new era of forgiveness, love and grace (Luke 4:18-19).

Therefore, we, who became Jesus' disciples, should do the same work as Jesus. Jesus said:
> *"He who believes in me will do the same things that I do. He*

will do even greater things than these because I am going to the Father." (John 14:12)

We must cast out devils and rescue those suffering souls from the bondage of devils and lead them to God. As the seventy disciples of Jesus rejoiced after they preached the gospel powerfully and reported back to Jesus, we too should taste that same joy:

"Lord, even the demons obeyed us when we used your name!" (Luke 10:17)

The Attitudes of a Disciple

To do the works of Jesus, we as His disciples should take note of several attitudes very clearly.

First, a disciple of Jesus should be totally a Jesus-man. Jesus said,
"If any man will come after me, let him deny himself, and take up his cross, and follow me." (Matthew 16:24 AV)

Once we have become Jesus' disciples we should no longer say, "My...." "My...." We should now discard "my pride", "my wish", "my greediness", and completely thrust ourselves upon Jesus. In "my home", "my business", "my whole life", we should let Jesus be our master. We should also *"take up the cross"* of Jesus, as the Authorized Version puts it.

Taking up our cross means to work at proclaiming the eternal love of Jesus, who loves us sinners and died on the cross to make atonement for our sins.

When we live as Jesus' disciples, there will be times when we are mocked by the devil and persecuted, but it should not bother us because the battle we are fighting has already been won by Jesus.

Denying ourselves, we will make a firm resolution to follow Jesus only, preach His words only, carrying the cross of glory and victory.

Second, a disciple should be wise and pure (Matthew 10:16-23). Even if the wicked stirred up by Satan should persecute us, we should give thanks to God because the glory of God will be manifested through the persecution. We should continue to witness to the Word of God under the guidance of the Holy Spirit. Jesus gave His word for those who speak when under persecution:

"It will not really be you speaking. The Spirit of your Father will be speaking though you." (Matthew 10:20)

We, Jesus' disciples, should witness to the good news of the kingdom of God in the power of the Holy Spirit at any time, anywhere, with a shrewd but gentle mind.

Third, a disciple of Jesus should endure. The Word of God promised:

> *Those who cry as they carry out the seeds will return singing and carrying bundles of grain.* (Psalm 126:5)

Whether a proper time is given to us or not, we must proclaim the good news about the kingdom of God by enduring any kind of circumstance (2 Timothy 4:2).

When we lead one soul to salvation, a joyous heavenly feast is held in the kingdom of God. In remembrance of this fact, we should not be tardy nor discouraged in our duty of winning souls.

CLOSING QUESTIONS

Whom shall we teach?
(Matthew 28:19)

What are the three steps to becoming Jesus' disciples?
(Matthew 16:24)

a. _____

b. _____

c. _____

What signs will follow believers?
(Mark 16:17-18)

APPLICATION

1. As Jesus' disciples, let us become faithful workers for the Lord.

2. To work faithfully in the area that is entrusted to us, let us always seek the help of the Holy Spirit.

3. Let us obey and act upon the word of Jesus as Peter did.

JESUS PERFORMS
MIRACLES

1. **Today's Scripture**
   John 2:1-11
2. **Memory Verse**
   John 2:5
   > *His mother said to the servants, "Do whatever he tells you to do."*
3. **Reference Scripture**
   Matthew 7:7-11
4. **Objectives**
   a. Let us realise that Jesus is performing miracles for us today too.
   b. Let us become obedient Christians to Jesus.
   c. Let us become believers who strive to give, rather than only receive.

LEADING QUESTIONS

> ### Where did Jesus perform His first miracle?
> (John 2:11)

> ### With what did Jesus tell them to fill the waterpots?
> (John 2:7)

> ### Who was commended by the people for the best wine, which Jesus made?
> (John 2:9-11)

TODAY'S MESSAGE

Being invited, Jesus went to a wedding feast in Cana. As the banquet was at the height of merriment, they ran out of wine. From the very beginning of their new married life, the bridegroom and bride were put into a very awkward position. But through Jesus, this couple received the solution to their impending problem. Like them, we also meet with all kinds of trouble as we live on this earth. What shall we do when we are in trouble? We will see and receive the answer through the miracle experience of this young couple when they were with Jesus.

The Newly Wedded Couple's Frustration

The first lesson we must learn from this couple is their attitude. Their first trouble was facing a big embarrassment because they had prematurely run out of wine in the climax of their joyous wedding feast. But instead of retreating to a corner, downhearted with despair, they stood up to find a solution to their problem. They brought the matter to Jesus' mother and she took it to Jesus.

On this earth no one is living without problems. But there are winners and losers because their heart attitudes are different when they run against difficulties. Your attitude can lead you to the road of success or down a road to failure.

Most people, when they encounter life's obstacles, say: "Something serious has happened to me. Oh, I am in trouble! What can I do!" As soon as people utter such words a sense of insecurity and fear begins to spark a flame in their heart, soon they are engulfed in a negative attitude and eventually they enter the road to destruction. But against exactly the same problem, there are people who say: "Something serious has happened to me. Very well! I'll confront it!" And these few will become the winners who live on the road of success.

Joshua and Caleb, among the twelve spies sent out to the Canaan land, are good examples. When they encountered a problem, they chose the attitude of "Very well, we can take the city!" That is how they could report in such positive faith:

> "Don't turn against the Lord! Don't be afraid of the people in that land! We will chew them up." (Numbers 14:9)

Man cannot survive without bread – and Joshua and Caleb took their serious problem as their bread, with the attitude of obtaining new strength even by eating up the very problem they encountered. How marvellous was their thought!

There is no one in the world who ever encountered a problem that was more serious than the one Jesus met. When Jesus was praying at the Mount of Olives, the officers and the chief priests came to arrest Him. Peter immediately thought: "I've got a problem. I am in trouble!" and in confusion struck the right ear of the high priest's servant. Then Jesus told Peter to put his sword back into the sheath and said:

> "Shall I not drink of the cup the Father has given me?"

Jesus accepted His "problem" and drank the cup of suffering, the "crucifixion on the cross". By Jesus' obedience to the problem, He became the door of blessing for every sinner to be forgiven of his sins, healed of sickness, freed from curse and to obtain life from death.

Likewise, we should not become discouraged and sink down when a problem comes to us. Rather we should give thanks to God for the problem because when we do so, it will take off its mask and its true face, God's purpose for allowing it, will turn out to be a blessing in disguise.

The frustrating problem of running out of wine at the wedding banquet turned out to become a doorway to a great blessing. The whole thing could have turned out to be a failure because wine had run out in the peak of the festivities, but this couple, with a positive attitude, anticipated a solution and brought the matter to Jesus' mother who sought Jesus' solution. This was how Jesus' first miracle came about. And the couple's wedding banquet was so blessed that their story became part of our Bible story for thousands of years for the children of God.

They Invited Jesus When They Had Food

The second point we note from this couple is that they did invite Jesus and His disciples to their banquet. This couple who were just married could experience God's miracle because they had invited Jesus when they had food to treat Him. I urge you believers, too, to treat Jesus well. Whenever you can, give your time and money to Jesus as taught in Matthew 7:12:
> *"Do for other people the same things you want them to do for you. This is the meaning of the law of Moses and the teaching of the prophets."*
We always want Jesus to do things for us first while we want to do things for Jesus last. This is the wrong order. When I am able to give, I must give to God. That which I give will be deposited in heaven and God will return it to me in an answered prayer when I need Him.

They Obeyed

The third attitude we should learn from this couple is their obedience. When Jesus' mother told Him that wine had run out, He said:
> *"Dear woman, why come to me? My time has not yet come."*
We should learn from this that when Jesus blesses us He always does it according to His timing.

Jesus never comes too late or too early. He always arrives on time. As we worship the Lord and wait upon Him, when His time is fulfilled, He will speak to us and once the word of the Lord comes to us, the problem is solved.

Mary knew this so she told the servants:

"Do whatever he tells you to do."

Jesus, in His own time, gave His command:

"Fill the jars with water!"

The servants, in obedience to Jesus' command, filled them up to the brim. Then Jesus commanded:

"Now take some out and give it to the master of the feast."

When they faithfully obeyed His command, water became wine! Their problem became a blessing, the very best blessing! The word from the governor of the feast, *"you have saved the best wine till now"*, proves it was the best wine of the day, which is also a very significant point. What the world is giving you may taste good at the beginning but it will taste bitter in the end. But what Jesus is giving you seems to be bitter at first, but in the long run you will find that anything from Jesus will not only be good but will be the best blessing for you!

Jesus wants to give us good things. Jesus is our good Lord so He changes our problem to become the wine of joy.

Do you feel yourself to be as worthless as water? Even so, give yourself to Jesus and let Him take charge of you. Then your life will become like the best wine, that is welcomed by all people, and will contribute to their benefit!

CLOSING QUESTIONS

According to Joshua and Caleb, what was the problem? (Numbers 14:9)

What did Jesus say was the meaning of "the law of Moses and the teaching of the prophets?" (Matthew 7:12)

After Jesus performed the miracle, how did the master of the wedding commend the bridegroom? (John 2:10)

Now consider the application of this lesson which you will find on the next page.

APPLICATION

1. When we encounter a difficulty, this is the time for Jesus to perform a miracle for us. Let us have this kind of positive faith.

2. By obeying Jesus, we can experience God's miracles.

JESUS CLEANSES
THE TEMPLE

1. **Today's Scripture**
   John 2:13-22
2. **Memory Verse**
   John 2:19
   > *Jesus answered, "Destroy this temple, and I will build it again in three days."*
3. **Reference Scripture**
   Matthew 21:12-13
4. **Objectives**
   a. We, who are God's temples, must purify ourselves and exert all of our efforts to live a clean life through continuous prayer. (1 Corinthians 3:16)
   b. We must give thanks to Jesus who shed His blood for our sake and died on the cross.

LEADING QUESTIONS

> **What kind of place did Jesus say we should not make His Father's house?**
> (John 2:16)

> **How many days did Jesus say it would take to raise His temple if it were destroyed?**
> (John 2:19)

> **How many years did it take to build the temple?**
> (John 2:20)

TODAY'S MESSAGE

Jesus purified the temple twice. John chapter 2 records the first time and Matthew chapter 21 records the second purification. This lesson will deal with Jesus cleansing the temple and how it relates to us now in how we follow God's will.

My House is the House of Prayer

Jesus went up to the temple in Jerusalem to observe the Passover.

201

But the holy temple where people should have been worshipping God had become a noisy market-place, full of money changers and vendors selling animals for sacrifice such as oxen, sheep or doves. Seeing this, Jesus made a scourge of small cords and drove them out saying:

> *"Don't make my Father's house a place for buying and selling!"* (John 2:16)
>
> *"It is written in the Scriptures, 'My Temple will be a house where people will pray.' But you are changing God's house into a 'hideout for robbers.'"* (Matthew 21:13)

In those days, merchandisers sold animals for sacrifice and money changers exchanged money for the Jews who returned to Jerusalem from abroad to observe the Passover feast. Jewish men above twenty years of age were required to pay half a shekel for temple tax, but in those days the Roman currency was the prevailing currency, so they had to change their money to shekels. These merchandisers and money changers were profiteering excessively, in collusion with corrupt high priests of the temple. Those priests even deliberately found fault with the animals brought by the native Jews to force them to buy again from the vendors who were connected with them in profiteering. The people's grievances resounded high in Jerusalem because of the profane merchandising activities in the holy temple.

When He saw the worship that was to be lifted in spirit and truth becoming perverted into religious rituals, and the temple being blemished by those vendors, Jesus, in the solemn authority of the triune God, the worship recipient, drove them out of the temple. He saw the people's corrupt attitude and actions, through their negligent preparation of sacrifice animals. In the temple, no voice of prayer and praise was heard. No repenting tears from contrite hearts were seen. Instead, only the sound of commotion from the noisy animal cries filled the temple. Jesus had to take the whip to clean His temple.

Today our Lord Jesus is in the Church, His body, and He speaks to us today too:

> *"God is spirit. Those who worship God must worship in spirit and truth."* (John 5:24)

When we worship the Lord God with purified lips and heart He will accept our worship.

Therefore, we must acknowledge the Holy Spirit, welcome His presence and usher Him into our hearts so that He will fill us and purify us. Let us remember what Jesus said:

"My Temple will be a house where people will pray."
Let us build the altar of prayer, love the Word of God and act upon the Word of God so that we will become holy and glorious temples of God in the place where He loves to dwell.

Jesus in Jerusalem for the Passover

From the time He was twelve years old, Jesus went up to Jerusalem at the feast of the Passover every year in accordance with the law (Luke 2:41-42). After He was baptized by John He had observed the Passover feast four times. During the fourth Passover, Jesus drank the bitter cup of death on the cross. The purification of the temple which we are studying now took place six months after He was baptized by John the Baptist.

The origin of the Passover feast, as already seen in Unit 3, Lesson 21, was as follows. To deliver the people of Israel from Egypt, God sent a plague which killed the firstborn of every Egyptian family, from the palace right down to the servants' homes. But all the Israelites were saved by putting the blood of the Passover lamb on the lintel and doorposts of their homes. They ate the roasted lamb according to their instructions and escaped from Egypt (Exodus chapter 12). To remember the exodus from the land of bondage, the feast of Passover was observed in Israel; it is one of the three most important Jewish feasts, the other two being the feast of weeks or the Pentecost (Deuteronomy 16:10,16) and the feast of shelters or tabernacles (Leviticus 23:34, 42-43). To observe this feast of Passover, Jesus went up to Jerusalem.

What is the relation between the Passover feast and Jesus Christ?
Jesus came as the baby lamb for all humanity. He became the sacrifice lamb to bear all the sins of mankind. Jesus was without blemish. Jesus was the spotless Son of God, yet He came clothed in flesh, shed blood and allowed His flesh to be torn so the power of death, like the plague, could "pass over" all of us. Therefore, believing in Jesus means believing in the power of His blood that forgives our sins and makes us righteous to become children of God through the work of the Holy Spirit.

As He started His public ministry, Jesus went up to Jerusalem to observe the feast of Passover. This has a deep meaning because in His heart He desired eagerly that all who believe in Him should be cleansed by the price of His blood, the sacrifice Passover lamb.

Destroy This Temple

Seeing Jesus rebuking the merchandisers, the Jewish people questioned:

> *"Show us a miracle for a sign. Prove that you have the right to do these things."*

The Jews thought maybe this person came as Messiah and they wanted to see the sign that He was indeed Messiah. Jesus answered them:

> *"Destroy this temple, and I will build it again in three days."*

By this, He meant that He would be crucified on the cross, buried and resurrected in three days.

When Jesus was asked by the same Pharisees and scribes to show the Messianic sign, He took the sign of the prophet Jonah and foretold of His death and resurrection (Matthew 12:39-40).

The first temple in Jerusalem was built by Solomon but destroyed later by King Nebuchadnezzar in BC 586. It was restored later by Nehemiah and Esther. But King Herod rebuilt the temple and it was called Herod's temple. Magnificently glittering with golden colours, the Jews thought of the temple as their pride and joy. But they took no interest in *worshipping God* in the temple, because they were preoccupied only with their religious rituals. Thus a high wall of sin, hypocrisy, disobedience and distrust stood between the Jews and God. Jesus was God Who came to break this wall so that He can meet His people in the relationship of love.

Nevertheless, because all men are sinners, in their own strength no one can go forward to God. Without the badge of "sin-forgiven", he cannot see God. So Jesus came, allowed His flesh to be torn, His body to be destroyed and provided the way that we may come to God. He destroyed the old covenant and built the new covenant of faith with His shed blood and torn flesh.

In summary, we who believe in Jesus, Who purified the temple, should also purify ourselves first, as temples of God, and then we should strive to live holy lives. We must praise Jesus, the Passover lamb, both in our living and at our worship services. Let us rely always on the power of Jesus' blood and dwell in Jesus-given new life. His resurrection is my resurrection!

CLOSING QUESTIONS

> ### What did Jesus mean when He said He would build the temple again in three days?
> (John 2:21)

> ### What kind of house did Jesus call His temple?
> (Matthew 21:13)

> ### List the three most important feasts of the Jewish people.
> (Find the answer from today's message.)

APPLICATION

1. God's house is the house of prayer. Do you always pray when you wake? Let us always build the altar of our prayer to God.

2. As Jesus taught, *"Those who worship God must worship in spirit and truth"* (John 5:24), let us always prepare our heart in spirit and in truth before we worship our Heavenly Father.

JESUS WORKS ON
THE SABBATH

1. **Today's Scripture**
   Matthew 12:1-21
2. **Memory Verse**
   Matthew 12:8
   "The Son of Man is Lord of the Sabbath day."
3. **Reference Scripture**
   Mark 2:23-3:5, Luke 13:10-17
4. **Objectives**
   a. Let us always observe the Lord's holy day.
   b. Let us realize that Jesus worked on the Sabbath just as He works today and every day.
   c. Let us live a life of worshipping Jesus on the Sabbath and every day, returning all the glory to Him.

LEADING QUESTIONS

> **How was Jesus compared to the temple?**
> (Matthew 12:6)

> **What did Jesus want more than animal sacrifices?**
> (Matthew 12:7)

> **Who is Lord of the Sabbath day?**
> (Matthew 12:8)

TODAY'S MESSAGE

The Old Testament's Sabbath day was to commemorate God's resting after He completed the creation of the heaven, the earth, all things in it and mankind. The Bible says:
Remember to keep the Sabbath as a holy day.... The reason is that in six days the Lord made everything. He made the sky, earth, sea and everything in them. And on the seventh day, he rested. (Exodus 20:8, 11)
It was 24 hours from Friday sunset to the same time on Saturday. Since New Testament days, we now observe Jesus' resurrection day as the Lord's day for worshipping, which is the first after the old Sabbath. Today, we will study the things that Jesus did on the Sabbath.

207

Jesus Taught on the Sabbath

On the Sabbath, Jesus went into the synagogue in Nazareth and read and taught the book of Isaiah. In Capernaum, He also taught people in the synagogue, and people were astonished by His teaching. Jesus' teachings were different from those of the scribes, and His teachings were also full of authority. His teachings shook the hearts of listeners because Jesus' Word was God's Word as Jesus was a member of the triune Godhead.

Jesus came to this earth, preached the good news of the kingdom of God and taught. He taught the goodness of God and the truth of salvation, that we receive eternal life by believing in Him. He also taught that the devil's work is to rob, kill and destroy us, but that the Holy Spirit is always helping us.

Even today, God's Word is taught on the Lord's day. Jesus, through His chosen servants, is still letting us know the news about the kingdom of God. Paul taught Timothy, his son in faith:

> *Be careful in your life and in your teaching. Continue to live and teach rightly. Then you will save yourself and those people who listen to you.* (1 Timothy 4:16)

Jesus commanded:

> *"Teach them to obey everything I have told you."* (Matthew 28:20)

When the Word of God is heard today, preached in the power of the Holy Spirit, it will become powerful enough to divide our soul and spirit, to keep us holy and with the discipline to walk in the truth of the Word.

Jesus Did Good Things on the Sabbath

Once when Jesus was teaching on the Sabbath in a synagogue, a man with an evil spirit shouted:

> *"Jesus of Nazareth! What do you want with us?"* (Mark 1:24)

Here, calling Him as "Jesus of Nazareth", Satan tried to cause the Jews to belittle Jesus because the Jewish people used to despise the Nazarenes. But Jesus rebuked the evil spirit:

> *"Be quiet! Come out of the man!"*

The evil spirit came out instantly. As we have seen here, Jesus both taught and healed on the Sabbath.

On another Sabbath, Jesus healed a man with a withered hand and the Jewish leader accused Him of breaking the Sabbath by healing the man on that day. Then Jesus answered them:

> *"Which is right on the Sabbath day: to do good, or to do evil?"* (Mark 3:4)

Jesus came to this world to fulfil God's good will. His good will is to rescue the death-doomed sinners, save them, give them a new life, and make them His children so that they can prosper in all things and be in health, just as their souls prosper.

While teaching on the Sabbath in a synagogue, Jesus healed a demon-possessed woman who had been a cripple for eighteen years. This woman glorified God immediately but the ruler of the synagogue was angered:

"There are six days for work. So come to be healed on one of those days. Don't come for healing on the Sabbath day."

And Jesus answered:

"All of you untie your work animals and lead them to drink water every day – even on the Sabbath day! This woman that I healed is our Jewish sister. But Satan has held her for 18 years. Surely it is not wrong for her to be freed from her sickness on a Sabbath day!" (Luke 13:14)

Today, too, Jesus dwells in the church through the Holy Spirit. When we gather together to worship Him and honour His name, He does the same work for us as He did during His earthly ministry. Some Christians, even though they have been born again, still live in disbelief and lead the life of a slave to sin, Satan and sickness. When we worship the Lord God and honour His name, Satan is loosened from his stronghold.

Jesus is Lord of the Sabbath

The Israelites observed the Sabbath as the day of worshipping and the day of rest (Leviticus 23:3). But after they returned from the Babylonian captivity, the Sabbath became blurred to them and their activities became rituals. Their Sabbath turned into an instrument of their hypocrisy.

To such legalistically minded Jews, Jesus taught the true meaning of the Sabbath. The Sabbath is for man. The day following Adam's creation was the Sabbath. His first full day was the day of rest in the blessed garden that God had provided for him. Note here that the Sabbath was a day of peace, joy and rest for Adam, not a day of bondage, captivity and pressure. The only thing Adam was required to do on that day was to praise God and worship Him.

Jesus came into Bethlehem, Judea, to be the Saviour of His people. Through His shed blood and wounded body on the cross, Jesus paid the death penalty and erased the original sin of mankind. From that awesome day, He quickens and gives eternal life to whoever believes in Him. This Jesus who gave us a new life, a new hope, a new chance to begin again, was resurrected on the first day after the Sabbath.

By disobeying God, Adam and Eve lost the peace of God. They were cursed by God and their spirits died. Consequently, everything concerning their lives went wrong, and their bodies began to know sickness. They were "cursed". Now they would have to shed blood and sweat to produce food and make their way in life to survive. But we who have become Christians by believing Jesus and obeying Him have now entered a new eternal Sabbath. We gather together, on the day commemorating Jesus' resurrection, to worship Him and He gives us peace. The early church worshipped the Lord on the first day after the Sabbath (Acts 2:1, 20:7) which was the day of Jesus' resurrection. The Apostle Paul also recommended that we worship the Lord on the first day of the week (1 Corinthians 16:1, 2).

Jesus answered the Pharisees:
"The Son of Man is Lord of the Sabbath day." (Matthew 12:8) when they accused Jesus and His disciples of taking an ear of corn and eating it on the Sabbath. On the Sabbath the Triune God receives our worship and He bestows His peace and rest upon us.

Today, we were taught what Jesus did on the Sabbath and His continuing work among us. May all His mercy and love be upon us whenever we worship the Lord Jesus!

CLOSING QUESTIONS

> **Jesus' teaching was different from whose teaching?**
> (Mark 1:22)

> **Which one of the ten commandments is the commandment about the Sabbath?**
> (Exodus 20:8-11)

> **On which day did God rest when He created the world?**
> (Genesis 2:2,3)

Now consider the application of this lesson which you will find on the next page.

APPLICATION

1. Let us study the words of Jesus, live by the power of His word and lead a successful faith life.

2. Today we have learned about the Sabbath and Jesus' teaching that "it is good to do good things on the Sabbath". Am I doing good things for the needy neighbours who live near me? Share with one another about experiences of helping others.

JESUS
PRAYS

1. **Today's Scripture**
   Mark 1:35-39
2. **Memory Verse**
   Mark 1:35
   > *Early the next morning, Jesus woke and left the house while it was still dark. He went to a place to be alone and pray.*
3. **Reference Scripture**
   Matthew 6:5-13
4. **Objectives**
   a. Let us always strive to become fervent praying believers as Jesus was and still is praying today.
   b. Let us not stop praying for those we should lead to Jesus; our family members and our neighbours.

LEADING QUESTIONS

> ### When and where did Jesus pray?
> (Mark 1:35)

> ### After Jesus cast out the evil spirit what did He say was the only way to force this kind out?
> (Mark 9:29)

> ### What did Jesus do during the night before He chose His disciples?
> (Luke 6:12-16)

TODAY'S MESSAGE

Jesus is truly God and truly man Who came to this world. Jesus, as the sacrificial lamb for sinners, led a life of prayer. He prayed to be strengthened in power to break Satan's stronghold so that He could rescue sinners from the slavery of Satan. He prayed to praise God. He prayed to seek God's forgiveness towards sinners. Jesus prayed for the weak. The life of Jesus on earth was tied together with unceasing continuing prayer. Even now He is continuing His prayer ministry for us at the right hand of God.

Jesus Always Prayed

The first record of Jesus' prayer is in Luke 3:21. After He was baptized, He prayed to God once more and set His heart to obey God's will. The answer to Jesus' prayer came immediately. The Holy Spirit and a voice from heaven descended right away.

Before choosing his twelve disciples, Jesus prayed to God all through the night.

Jesus prayed before the daylight and always preached His kingdom powerfully throughout the day. When casting out evil spirits, He also used the power of prayer. Returning from the Mount of Transfiguration, Jesus healed a lunatic and taught His disciples:
    "This kind can only be forced out by prayer." (Mark 9:29)

Jesus always prayed to praise God. The praise songs we are giving the Lord are songs of our prayer.

Before Jesus called for Lazarus to come forth from his grave, He also prayed a prayer of thanksgiving and praise to His Father. Many of the Jews were present and Mary and Martha were watching too, full of awe. In front of the already impossible situation, Jesus prayed to the Father, lifting up his eyes:
    "Father, I thank you that you heard me. I know that you always hear me." (John 11:41, 42)

Jesus prayed to God when he fed thousands of people with five loaves and two fishes; He prayed for His disciples; He prayed at the garden of Gethsemane; He prayed on the cross:
    "Father, forgive them. They don't know what they are doing." (Luke 23:34)
His life was closed with His final prayer to His Father:
    "My God, my God, why have you left me alone?" (Matthew 27:46)

Jesus' life began in prayer and ended in prayer. Modelling our prayer life on Jesus, let us always pray and cast out evil spirits so that we lead a successful, well-balanced faith life.

What to Pray?

Jesus taught us what to pray and also gave us His good example of prayer.

First, Jesus told us to pray to receive the Holy Spirit. He promised

that the Comforter, the Holy Spirit, would be sent after He ascended to heaven. He taught us to pray to receive the Holy Spirit:
> *"Even though you are bad, you know how to give good things to your children. So surely your heavenly Father knows how to give the Holy Spirit to those who ask him."* (Luke 11:13)

As Jesus always prayed, the Holy Spirit was always present upon Him and by the power of the Holy Spirit He could cast out evil spirits and build the kingdom of God (Matthew 12:18). Therefore prayer is the royal road to walk on, together with the Holy Spirit and to receive His help.

Second, Jesus said:
> *"Stay awake and pray that you will not be tempted."* (Mark 14:38)

In order for us to cast out the devil, to overcome his evil temptation to recover sinners from Satan's slavery and for the kingdom of God, we must be armed with prayer.

As we pray, both our flesh and soul will be strengthened and our spirit will get enough power from the Lord to control our greed and lust of the flesh.

Third, Jesus requested us to pray for our brothers (Luke 22:32). Especially, as we pray for our brethren who are infants in the faith, our prayers prevent Satan from causing our weaker brethren to fail. We must pray also for the body of Christ, our Christian members.

Fourth, we should pray that God's will will be done. Jesus prayed:
> *"My Father, if it is possible, do not give me this cup of suffering. But do what you want, not what I want."* (Matthew 26:39)

The only One who always knows the right decision for our lives and our business is our heavenly Father! Therefore, our praying that God's will be done means we want the best result manifested at all times in our lives.

Fifth, Jesus taught:
> *"So be ready all the time. Pray that you will be strong enough to escape all these things that will happen. And pray that you will be able to stand before the Son of Man."* (Luke 21:36)

Our ultimate hope is not in this world. We are just travelling through this life. This world is not our final home. Our yearning is for the time we shall stand before Jesus Christ as His bride in the eternal kingdom of God. Therefore, till we reach the end of our lives on this earth and receive the crown of righteousness, we must not stop praying to our heavenly Father.

Answers to Prayer

Answers always follow prayer. Jesus promised His answered prayer to us in John 14:13:

> *"And if you ask for anything in my name, I will do it for you. Then the Father's glory will be shown through the Son."*

> *"Until now you have not asked for anything in my name. Ask and you will receive. And your joy will be the fullest joy."* (John 16:24)

> *"If you believe you will get anything you ask for in prayer."* (Matthew 21:22)

God always hears the prayers of those who cry out to Him and He always answers them. The Holy Spirit also helps our infirmities:
> *"We do not know how to pray as we should. But the Spirit Himself speaks to God for us, even begs God for us. The Spirit speaks to God with deep feelings that words cannot explain."* (Romans 8:26)

Let us follow Jesus' prayer and pray always too!

CLOSING QUESTIONS

What is the reason that God does not answer our prayer? (Psalm 66:18)

What must we do to be forgiven of our sins by God? (1 John 1:9)

How can we obtain strength against temptation? (Luke 22:46)

Now consider the application of this lesson which you will find on the next page.

APPLICATION

1. Generally, we should pray as follows:
   a. praise God
   b. confess our sins
   c. give Him thanks for blessings already received
   d. ask for what we need
   e. conclude with thanks in faith for His answer to our prayer.

   You may try to pray in this manner.

2. When praying, Jesus often laboured very hard. Even if we do not receive answers to prayer immediately, let us continue in faith and persist in prayer and patience.

JESUS CONQUERS
DEATH

1. **Today's Scripture**
   John 11:33-44
2. **Memory Verse**
   John 11:40
   Jesus said to her, "Didn't I tell you that if you believed, you would see the glory of God?"
3. **Reference Scripture**
   Luke 7:11-17
4. **Objectives**
   a. Let us understand correctly Jesus Christ's power to conquer death at any time.
   b. Let us always remember His command to those standing by at the raising of Lazarus:
      "Take the cloth off of him and let him go."
      In the AV it reads:
      "Loose him, and let him go."
      Today he is speaking this very same command to us.
   c. No matter how difficult and quickly circumstances or tests try to overwhelm us, let us stand firm and become "Christians who fear not, but only believe."

LEADING QUESTIONS

Jesus said to Martha and Mary:
"He who believes in me will have life even if he dies."
(John 11:25, 26).
How could he say this?

What did Jesus do and say when He looked at Lazarus' tomb?
(John 11:41-43)

What did Jesus command the people to do for Lazarus after he came out, bound hand and foot with graveclothes?
(John 11:44)

TODAY'S MESSAGE

Jesus has greater power than any religious leader, revolutionist, or philosopher of the world could have. It is because He is the only One Who thoroughly conquered death. Throughout human history, there have been many great religions, philosophies, great ideas for social reformation or revolutions, but none of their leaders have been able to conquer death. Only Jesus perfectly overpowered and conquered death.

Jesus Raises the Dead

In the four books of the gospel, there are three instances of Jesus miraculously raising the dead.

Though Lazarus' decomposed body had already begun to stink, Jesus commanded: *"Lazarus, come out!"* and the dead Lazarus came back to life and walked out of the tomb.

The Bible says the wages of sin is death. When Adam and Eve fell, a curse fell on all humanity. Man was sentenced to death for the price of sin. But Jesus came to give us life. While He was on earth, there was not a single instance where He ever preached a funeral sermon, but He brought life to those who had died. Jesus gave us resurrection life too, when we were born again. Jesus Christ is the only name through Whom we must be saved.

Lazarus, Come Out!

Beside Lazarus' dead body, Mary and Martha, his sisters, were sobbing with grief because they had leaned on Lazarus heavily since their parents' early death. Mary and Martha would not have spared their lives for their brother's sake if it had been necessary, but their fervent love was of no use because he was dead. In the middle of their grief, Jesus spoke life-giving words, *"Lazarus, come out!"* and Lazarus rose and walked about of his tomb in his burial clothes.

Since the transgression of Adam and Eve against God, all their descendants have been living in the tomb of the flesh. Man has been living without knowing where he came from, why he is living and where he is heading. Who would quicken our dead spirits? The only One Who can quicken spiritually dead mankind is Jesus Christ, Who came to this world clothed in flesh, died on the cross and was resurrected after three days. When you take the words of Jesus: *"Lazarus, come out!"* into your heart, you can also be quickened from the dead state as Lazarus was raised. Lazarus came alive not by the

Jewish laws nor because of his sister's fervent love, but by the commanding words of Jesus. Likewise, the only One Who will save us today is Jesus Christ.

Take Off the Grave Clothes and Let Him Go

Jesus raised Lazarus, but He did not help in taking off the burial clothes when he walked out of the tomb. He instead commanded the people:

> *"Loose him and let him go."* (John 11:44 in the AV)

because taking off the past burial clothes is man's responsibility. In like manner, though we are saved by the grace of Christ, the job of taking off our old garment is ours. If we want to walk freely we must loosen the bondage of sin, the curse, the devil, poverty and other incumbrances. In other words, we are responsible for making our situation to prosper, so we can enjoy more abundantly the new life we have already received. We are the ones to carry out this job. The more "old garments" we take off, the more we will enjoy our salvation.

Now, let us study how we can loosen various kinds of bondage.

First, we must loosen our thinking.

We are to walk freely by breaking the ties of sin, sickness and death that have been binding us. When we are not walking freely, it makes Jesus sad. Therefore by the power of Jesus' cross, and using the authority He gave us, we must boldly cut off the bondage of sin consciousness, poverty consciousness and sickness consciousness; we should renew our minds with the thoughts: "I am forgiven! I am healed! I have obtained eternal life, so I am a winner!" and confess these facts through our lips.

Second, we must free ourselves from the bondage of anxiety and fear. Not knowing about the future, some people fear when they think of it. When life's problems attack and seem insoluble, people become easily oppressed by fear. But Jesus gave us His Word and Spirit so that we can overcome the enemy of anxiety and fear. When we hear God's Good News, faith comes in our heart (Romans 10:17), and when faith comes, a sense of insecurity and fear will leave us and God will work His miracle through our faith.

Third, we must free ourselves from a pessimistic or negative habit of language. In our daily living, we carelessly say: "It doesn't work" or "I am a failure", "I am finished", "I would die if ....", "I am not worthy" or "I can't do it." These words are the greatest enemies that destroy us. We must take off the garment of pessimistic and negative speech. We should always use positive, creative, active and lively words.

Fourth, Jesus not only said, *"Take the cloth off of him"* but He also said, *"let him go."* Our Lord Jesus does not want us to stick in one place, not advancing farther. If anyone says, "Yes, I believe" but does not act upon what he says he believes, that faith is a dead faith. Through the words of the scriptures, Jesus changes our minds and enables us to speak positive and creative words because He desires our lives to be full of God's miracles.

Lazarus came alive. He was set free from the grave clothes that bound him and returned home rejoicing, hand in hand with his sisters. There was joy instead of tears, praise instead of sighs, songs instead of mourning. Lazarus enjoyed his life abundantly at his home, at his work, and wherever he went. This is the life Jesus wants for all of us!

Even today, Jesus is with us to quicken dead spirits and free us from the curse.

CLOSING QUESTIONS

Why shouldn't we use negative words as believers? (Proverbs 18:21)

After all, what was the purpose of Lazarus' sickness? (John 11:4)

When the Spirit of God, Who raised Jesus from the dead, dwells in us, what will He give life to in us? (Romans 8:11)

Now consider the application of this lesson which you will find on the next page.

APPLICATION

1. Every day let us strive to restrain ourselves from speaking negative words. Let us change our habits of language so that we will always use active and positive words.

2. Let us cast out fear and anxiety by the power of the Word of God and the Holy Spirit. Let us always heed God's Word and grow in faith.

3. Let us become believers who have faith that acts upon the Word which says:
   "Take the cloth off of him and let him go."

JESUS BEARS OUR
SICKNESS

1. **Today's Scripture**
   Matthew 8:16
2. **Memory Verse**
   Matthew 8:17
   > *He did these things to make come true what Isaiah the prophet said:*
   > *"He took our suffering on him. And he felt our pain for us."*
3. **Reference Scripture**
   Isaiah 53:5-6
   1 Peter 2:21-25
4. **Objectives**
   a. Let us realize that about two-thirds of Jesus' earthly ministry was spent in healing the sick. The scriptures also declare Jesus always hates sickness and disease.
   b. Because the foundation of the kingdom of God is in healing, let us allow the blessing of God's healing to be bestowed daily upon our lives.

LEADING QUESTIONS

> ### What is the basis of our being healed?
> (1 Peter 2:24)

> ### What did Jesus take upon Himself in our stead?
> (Matthew 8:17)

> ### After He was resurrected, what five signs did Jesus tell His disciples would follow those who believed? Please list them in order from Mark 16:17-18.
>
> 1. _____
> 2. _____
> 3. _____
> 4. _____
> 5. _____

TODAY'S MESSAGE

Jesus came to this world as the greatest physician in human history. Two-thirds of His public ministry was spent in healing the sick. To us living in the world today this Jesus bestows the same healing grace. We will now study the Jesus Who bore our sickness, to heal us.

The Prophecy by Isaiah

The prophet Isaiah had described the scene of Jesus' suffering even more clearly than an actual eye-witness who later saw the crucifixion. Through Chapter 53, Isaiah gives us a full account of the gospel of healing. As we read in Isaiah 53:4:

But he took our suffering on him and felt our pain for us. We saw his suffering. We thought God was punishing him.

As these words declare, Jesus actually bore our sickness in His own body on the cross and suffered the grief, sorrow and pain from that sickness, in our stead.

Jesus Bore Our Sickness

What kind of sickness did Jesus heal and bear?

The Bible says the things that Jesus did were too many to record in all the books of the world (John 21:25). But if we try to name some of the ills Jesus healed, they are: skin disease or leprosy (Matthew 8:2-3), paralysis (Matthew 8:6), dropsy (Luke 14:2-4), fever (Matthew 8:14), constant bleeding (Matthew 9:20-22), blindness (Matthew 9:27-30), dumbness (Matthew 9:32-33), deafness (Mark 7:32-35), a crippled hand (Matthew 12:10), the lame (Matthew 15:30) and so on. Also, He delivered those who were possessed by evil spirits, those who had epilepsy and then healed them. All kinds of diseases and sicknesses were healed by Jesus Christ.

The Bible records that Jesus healed all kinds of sick people, including those who were despised and held in contempt by other people.

The Apostle Peter testified in Acts 10:38 how Jesus healed:

"You know about Jesus from Nazareth. God made him the Christ by giving him the Holy Spirit and power. You know how Jesus went everywhere doing good. He healed those who were ruled by the devil, because God was with Jesus."

By declaring:

> *"But if I use the power of God's Spirit to force out demons, this shows that the kingdom of God has come to you."* (Matthew 12:28)

Jesus Himself clearly showed us that the presence of the kingdom of God and the manifestation of healing are not separable. The presence of the kingdom of God inevitably brings healing. The foundation of the kingdom of God is in healing. So the Messiah, the builder of the kingdom of heaven, should necessarily become a physician for the sick also.

Are you in the kingdom of God? If so, you have entered into His blessing for healing and deliverance also, because Jesus is our Great Physician.

The Reason for Jesus Bearing our Sickness

Why did Jesus heal the sick, work signs and wonders and why is He still doing the same work today?

Some claim Jesus is healing and working miracles to prove that He is Messiah. This of course is an authentic view but it does not explain to the fullest extent the reason for Jesus' healing and miracles.

Another important reason that Jesus healed the sick was to show His loving kindness and mercy towards us. Wherever He went during His earthly ministry, He felt compassion toward sick and spirit-possessed people so He freed and healed them.

> *When Jesus arrived, he saw a large crowd. He felt sorry for them and healed those who were sick.* (Matthew 14:14)

> *Jesus felt sorry for the man. So he touched him and said, "I want to heal you. Be healed!"* (Mark 1:41)

These verses reveal that Jesus' healing works were not only to prove that He was the Messiah. Wherever He went, Jesus healed the sick out of deep compassion and mercy towards them. Who would dare stop the work of our Lord Jesus' loving kindness and mercy?

Signs That Follow Believers

The cross of Jesus brought us miracles of healing.

For our sicknesses, Jesus was inflicted with many wounds and by those wounds we were healed (1 Peter 2:24). Our Great Physician,

Jesus, gave this word of promise after He was resurrected:

> *"Anyone who believes and is baptized will be saved. But he who does not believe will be judged guilty. And those who believe will be able to do these things as proof: They will use my name to force demons out of people. They will speak in languages they never learned. They will pick up snakes without being hurt. And they will drink poison without being hurt. They will touch the sick and the sick will be healed."* (Mark 16:16-18)

Jesus, Who is the same yesterday, today and forever, declared that we are given power to heal the lepers, the blind, the paralysed and the crippled in His Name. This is an amazing promise from Jesus that signs and miracles will follow to those who believe in Him.

Therefore, by holding fast to this faithful promise of Jesus who is always merciful, loving and kind, we, as believers, must experience Jesus' healing and miracles in our lives.

CLOSING QUESTIONS

Who will be made well by the prayer which is said with faith?
(James 5:15)

How did Jesus feel towards the crowd of sick people?
(Matthew 14:14)

Does the Bible record absolutely all of the miracles performed by Jesus?
(John 21:25)

APPLICATION

1. Let us take the word of God: *"We are healed because of his wounds"*, believe it and confess with our mouth, "By His wounds, I am healed!"

2. By believing the Word of God, *"the prayer that is said with faith will make the sick person well"*, let us pray for the healing of our families and friends.

JESUS CASTS OUT
DEVILS

1. **Today's Scripture**
   Matthew 17:14-20
2. **Memory Verse**
   Matthew 17:18
   > *Jesus gave a strong command to the demon inside the boy. Then the demon came out, and the boy was healed.*
3. **Reference Scripture**
   Mark 5:1-20
4. **Objectives**
   a. By studying about Jesus Who hated the devil and cast him out, let us follow His example, and resist the devil also.
   b. By knowing the nature and work of the devil, let us always be watchful so that we will not be deceived by him.
   c. Let us realize that we possess the authority to cast out devils in the name of Jesus, and use this authority in our daily lives.

LEADING QUESTIONS

> ### Why couldn't the disciples of Jesus cast out the demon?
> (Matthew 17:19-20)

> ### How much faith did Jesus say was needed so that "All things will be possible for you."?
> (Matthew 17:20)

> ### How long did it take Jesus to heal the epileptic boy?
> (Matthew 17:18)

TODAY'S MESSAGE

This world in which we are living has days of bright sunshine and nights of pitch-black darkness as well. Likewise, in the spiritual realm, while there exists God's world of light, there exists also the world of the devil, which is the headquarters of the forces of darkness. This world of evil spirits has a structure, with Lucifer the fallen archangel as its head who is ruling all the evil forces. At the next level are the fallen angels who fell with Lucifer when he opposed God. These are also called evil spirits. Lastly, there are the myriads of demons on the actual front line of the evil forces. They stand directly opposite to us. The power that approaches, trying to destroy us all the time, is the power of these devils.

These phenomena cannot be understood nor explained through human science or intelligence with the natural mind. The Bible clearly reveals this unseen world of devils to born-again Christian believers.

The Different Kinds of Devils

First, the Bible tells about **unclean spirits** (Matthew 10:1 in the AV). "Unclean spirits" occupy our minds through unclean thoughts. Just as the air that surrounds us now is unclean because of air pollution, today's mental and environmental atmosphere which surrounds us is also indescribably filthy and corrupt. Evidence that unclean spirits abound in the world today, contaminating our environment, is found in the unclean content of wordly music, movies, books, etc.

Second, the Bible tells us about **evil spirits** (1 Samuel 16:14). Evil spirits are a higher class of demons than unclean spirits. Evil spirits cause people to be anxious, restless and distressed, and lead men into mental chaos.

The third group the Bible tells us about are **lying spirits** (2 Chronicles 18:21 in the AV). When grasped by a lying spirit, people lie very easily, as if they are telling the truth. Having their conscience seared with a hot iron, it is difficult for such people to be saved.

Fourth, the Bible says there are **seducing spirits** (1 Timothy 4:1 in the AV). The seducing spirits might be also called religious spirits because they often make people fall into heresy and cause them to deny Jesus' sonship to God, etc.

Fifth, there are **spirits of divination** (Acts 16:16 in the AV). These spirits falsely tell people of their past and future and confuse them. These spirits work not only outside Christianity but also within it, wherever they receive attention.

Sixth, the Bible mentions devils that bring all kinds of sickness to man (Acts 10:38). Medically speaking, sickness means "disease-causing germs" which attach themselves to human bodies, destroying the body's normal function. The source of these disease germs is the devil of sickness.

Therefore, we are able to see that behind all filthy talk, anxiety, restlessness, mental disorder, lies, denying of Jesus, fortune-telling, various kinds of sickness and so on, these devils are working. Now let us study how Jesus dealt with these devils.

Jesus Cast Out Devils

The purpose of Jesus' coming to this world was to rescue man from the bondage of Satan's rule so that He gives him eternal life.

Before they fell, Adam and Eve were perfect people with a free will. According to their free will, they happily obeyed God and ruled the earth well as God had entrusted it to them. But once Adam and Eve obeyed Satan instead of obeying God, they fell and became servants of Satan.

Ever since then, Satan, ruling the power of the air, has controlled the minds of men so unceasingly that they have worshipped idols and slipped into the way of destruction; however, God, being a God of love and mercy, did not leave man in that condition. To accomplish His love, He sent His only begotten Son, Jesus, born in the flesh and crucified on the cross. So Jesus became a redemptive sacrifice to bear man's sin. Now, Satan can no longer claim man's sickness, curse, hatred and strife for the wages of man's sin. God's only begotten Son, Jesus, came to this world to destroy Satan and his works. Wherever He went, He cast out the devils and set men free from their bondage.

The Authority that Jesus Gave to Us

Jesus gave authority to cast out devils not only to the disciples of His day, but to us living today too. Because we have already been given this authority to cast out devils, the devils should leave. When we proclaim "It is written ....." and we command them to go in the name of Jesus, they should go! Jesus said in Mark 16:17-18:
> "And those who believe will be able to do these things as proof. They will use my name to force demons out of people. They will speak in languages they never learned. They will pick up snakes without being hurt. And they will drink poison without being hurt. They will touch the sick, and the sick will be healed."

He also promised in Luke 10:19:

> *"Listen! I gave you power to walk on snakes and scorpions. I gave you more power than the enemy has. Nothing will hurt you."*

The word "power" in this case has a significant meaning. Satan also has power but his power does not reach God's power. "Power" in the Greek is "dunamis", meaning dynamite. Jesus-given power in the Greek is "exousia" which is used to indicate authority over the "dunamis" power. Now let us find out the difference between power and authority.

Today cars move on the streets with great power and speed but once a policeman signals with his tiny finger, we can see all the speeding traffic stop at once to obey the policeman's order. What brought total obedience to the policeman? He has authority! Authority overrules power. And the Bible tells us that we are given this authority to control the power of the enemy. We can and must become men and women who live in the authority Jesus gave us. From now on, by using the authority Jesus shared with us, we should cast out evil spirits, lying spirits, seducing spirits, devils of sickness, as Jesus did, and live victorious Christian lives.

CLOSING QUESTIONS

Why did Jesus come to earth? (John 10:10)

What did Jesus give us to control all the power of the enemy? (Luke 10:19)

The Bible says the devil "goes around like a roaring lion looking for someone to eat". How should we "stand strong"? (1 Peter 5:8-9)

Now consider the application of this lesson which you will find on the next page.

APPLICATION

1. According to the word in 1 Peter 5:9, let us stand strong in our faith and refuse to give in to the devil.

2. Let us break free from our old selves and walk with Jesus in the abundant life and the authority He shared with us.

THE MINISTRY OF
JESUS CHRIST

PART TWO

Jesus' ministry was a series of sufferings. He worked so much yet lived poorly; He performed miracle after miracle for others, yet his body and heart were afflicted; He helped people yet He was killed by those whom He helped. Why should Jesus, Who is God Himself, have lived under such destitution and affliction. He lived like that for our sake. To redeem us from our curse and to change that curse to a life of blessing, He became the curse. He received the wounds to remove our affliction and sickness and to give us wholesome health. He willingly ended His life tragically on the cross to exchange our death for eternal life. But He was resurrected after three days and accomplished our salvation! That same ministry of Jesus is continuing today through the Holy Spirit.

The Ministry of Jesus Christ – Part Two

THE MIRACLE OF THE FIVE LOAVES AND TWO FISH

1. **Today's Scripture**
   John 6:1-15
2. **Memory Verse**
   John 6:11
   > *Then Jesus took the loaves of bread. He thanked God for the bread and gave it to the people who were sitting there. He did the same with the fish. He gave them as much as they wanted.*
3. **Reference Scripture**
   Luke 9:10-17
4. **Objectives**
   a. Let us become believers who always expect God's miracles and actually experience them like Andrew did.
   b. As the boy gave his small lunch of five loaves and two fish to Jesus, let us show our faith to Jesus by planting our seed faith.
   c. As Jesus taught the disciples to gather up the leftovers of the miracle food, let us also live without wasting anything.

LEADING QUESTIONS

> ### Who offered the five loaves and two fish to Andrew?
> (John 6:9)

> ### Who brought them to Jesus?
> (John 6:8-9)

> ### When the people saw the miracle, who did they say Jesus was?
> (John 6:14)

TODAY'S MESSAGE

The incident of five thousand men miraculously fed by only five loaves and two fish teaches us many things. Through this miracle, Jesus is teaching us that when we follow Him not only is our spirit saved but also our bodily needs will be met. We will study now the need for seed faith before we can experience Jesus' blessings for our daily needs even as our soul prospers.

The Disciples' Big Problem

As Jesus preached the good news about the kingdom of God, casting out devils and healing the sick, a great crowd always followed Him. The majority of the crowd who followed were poverty stricken or sick in body and needed comfort and healing desperately. When Jesus taught them they received peace and joy. They also witnessed with their own eyes how devils were cast out and how those who were oppressed and crippled were raised up. Often time passed more quickly than they realized when they were following Jesus and listening to His teachings.

Dinner time was approaching one day as Jesus concluded teaching, and His disciples faced a big problem because there were more than 5,000 hungry adult men, without even counting the women and children there. In the book of Mark, the disciples told Jesus:

> It was now late in the day. Jesus' followers came to him and said, "No one lives in this place. And it is already very late. Send the people away. They need to go to the farms and towns around here to buy some food to eat."

But Jesus answered:

> "You give them food to eat." (Mark 6:35-37)

Jesus could say this because he had the solution.

It is the same today. Jesus wants to help us when we are in trouble. Jesus does not say to us, "You take care of your own problems." He wants us to bring our problems to Him so that we receive the answer from Him and His abundant blessings. We must also have the firm faith that when we bring our problems to Jesus, He will solve them without fail. We must also have our seed faith planted, to show outwardly that we indeed trust Him.

Now, we will see how differently Andrew and Philip acted towards the same problem which needed a solution.

Philip's Faith and Andrew's Faith

Through this miracle of the five loaves and two fish, we can compare the different levels of faith of Philip and Andrew. They were both disciples of Jesus. They both encountered the same problem in the same wilderness. They both needed a solution. But Philip's faith could not bring about a miracle, whereas Andrew's faith did.

To test Philip, Jesus asked a question:

> "Where can we buy bread for all these people to eat?"

Though Philip had experienced Jesus' power and miracles so many times, his faith still remained calculating and scientific. So Philip lifted his eyes and saw a great crowd, calculated and then presented his estimate to Jesus:

"We would all have to work a month to buy enough bread for each person here to have only a little piece."

Philip only knew the fact that neither he nor the hungry crowd had that much money, so he reported to Jesus: "I cannot feed them; it is impossible." His calculation was accurate and scientific but no help at all towards producing miracle faith for Jesus. Philip's faith could not bring any solution for the hungry crowd.

But in that same wilderness, under the same crisis, another disciple of Jesus, Andrew, had believed that Jesus could do a miracle there. Andrew wanted to show his faith and did his best to search for the seed of faith to plant until he finally found a little boy's lunch box with five loaves and two fish.

Andrew brought these to Jesus, saying in effect: "Lord, these will never be enough but I believe that you will perform a great miracle." It was just a little seed, but Jesus accepted what he brought, thanked God and broke the bread. Because of Andrew's "seed faith" the broken bread increased each time it was broken until the great crowd was sufficiently fed. Jesus showed another miracle when He asked the disciples to go back and gather up the leftovers. It is possible no one taught that there would be leftovers but even the leftovers of the miracle amounted to twelve basketfuls.

The key to our life lies in our attitude. We, too, have many problems to solve. So let us have an Andrew's attitude toward our problems. Let's always remember, "If I bring my problem to Jesus, He always has the solution."

The Little Boy's Sacrifice

Behind this great miracle there was a little boy's faith. Giving up his meal of five loaves and two fish to Jesus must have been a great sacrifice to this little boy. Like other adults around, this growing boy must have been very hungry at the end of the day, too, but by giving his food to Jesus, this lad planted his meal as a seed of faith in Jesus. As Jesus blessed this little seed of faith, the miracle of feeding many thousands of people took place. There were even twelve basketfuls left over.

Another truth to be studied and learned here is that Jesus taught them to gather carefully what was left over. God's blessings for us are never meant to be wasted. We must take good care of His blessings given to us and use them to share with others in need. Anything that God has made for us should not be wasted.

CLOSING QUESTIONS

> ### Near which town did Jesus' miracle of five loaves and two fish happen?
> (Luke 9:10)

> ### How much food did Jesus give to the people?
> (Luke 9:17)

> ### Where did Jesus go alone after the miracle?
> (John 6:15)

1. Even in the midst of impossible-looking problems, let us always keep our positive attitude, like Andrew, that we have Jesus Who can always perform miracles in our life. Let us live positively under any circumstances, and act in faith.

2. Like the lad who gave up his meal, let us gladly give what we have to Jesus. We will live a life of abundant harvest as we sow.

PETER'S CONFESSION OF FAITH

1. **Today's Scripture**
   Matthew 16:13-20
2. **Memory Verse**
   Matthew 16:16
   Simon Peter answered, "You are the Christ, the Son of the living God."
3. **Reference Scripture**
   Luke 5:8
   John 21:15-17
4. **Objectives**
   a. Like the Apostle Peter, let us have a personal experience of truly meeting Jesus as our personal Saviour.
   b. Let us be filled with the Holy Spirit and become a powerful witness for Jesus like the Apostle Peter.

LEADING QUESTIONS

> ### Who did Peter think Jesus was?
> (Matthew 16:16)

> ### What did Jesus respond to Peter's confession of faith?
> (Matthew 16:17)

> ### Who had given Peter such a revelation that he could confess such a great faith?
> (Matthew 16:17)

TODAY'S MESSAGE

Peter was a fisherman living near Lake Galilee. Peter met Jesus through his brother Andrew before but only knew Him as a great teacher. One night Peter laboured all night on the sea but caught no fish at all. Visiting agonizing Peter, Jesus commanded him to cast his net into a different and deeper place. Peter obeyed Jesus' word, though he himself was one of the best fishermen in town with much experience and knowledge. Jesus' command sounded useless, yet Peter obeyed Jesus' command and experienced a great miracle which filled his empty boat full of fish.

Peter's Confession

When Peter saw this miracle, immediately he knelt down before Jesus and confessed:

"Go away from me, Lord. I am a sinful man!" (Luke 5:8)

He realized now that the man he had simply regarded as a good teacher was actually the miracle-working awesome Lord God. Peter immediately felt that he was a sinner and he could not dare to stand in Jesus' presence. So he begged Jesus to leave. But Jesus chose Peter because he made an honest confession about himself. Since then Peter became Jesus' best pupil, and lived a blessed life walking with Jesus.

Taking along His disciples, Jesus worked many miracles for the people and also cast out devils. The disciples certainly thought of Jesus as a great Messiah and a Saviour for the poor and the sick, people possessed by evil spirits, or sinners like tax collectors, but they did not realize Jesus as their own personal Saviour for themselves. But Jesus wanted to meet each one of them individually and become their personal Saviour.

Before entering Jerusalem, He asked the disciples when they were in Caesarea Philippi:

"Who do the people say I am?" They answered, "Some people say you are John the Baptist. Others say you are Elijah. And others say that you are Jeremiah or one of the prophets." Then Jesus asked them: "And who do you say I am?" Simon Peter answered: "You are the Christ, the Son of the living God." (Matthew 16:13-16)

"Christ" means "the anointed One". In Old Testament days, only the kings, priests and prophets were anointed, so Peter's confession meant, "You are my king of power, my priest to atone for my sin, and my truth to hold on to." For this confession, Jesus commended Peter's faith highly:

"You are blessed."

Peter's Mistake

Though Peter made a great confession, he soon made several mistakes because he immediately became conceited because of Jesus' praise. When Jesus told the disciples about His forthcoming suffering in Jerusalem, Peter rebuked Him:

"Those things will never happen to you!" (Matthew 16:22)

Out of his own human desire, Peter tried to stop Jesus from suffering on the cross.

By God's revelation, Peter understood the truth that Jesus is the Son of the living God and also His Saviour, but Peter did not know how Jesus could save people from their sins. Because Peter was ignorant of this truth, Satan stirred up Peter's heart so that he tried to stop Jesus' redemption work on the cross.

Not only that, when Jesus was arrested, Peter was overtaken by fear and followed Him from afar, even denying Him three times in the priest's courtyard. This same Peter who had sworn earlier that he would follow Jesus at the expense of his own life, now denied Jesus and even cursed Him (Matthew 26:69-75).

As Jesus' disciple, Peter was directly taught by Jesus, made a great confession of faith and experienced great miracles from Jesus, yet when he attempted to solve problems according to his own human desire and reasoning, he made grave mistakes and fell into despondency.

The Restoration of Peter

Seized with a consciousness of complete failure, Peter returned to his old job fishing in Galilee. The feeling of "I failed" must have pressed him more and more. But Jesus did not leave Peter alone in this pit of despair and frustration. He knew what Peter was going through so He visited Peter and performed the miracle of catching 153 fish for him, after a night when he had caught nothing (John 21:3-11). The blessings and miracles from Jesus always surpass our expectation. When we ruin things and are left alone, discouraged and despondent with no one capable of solving our problems, Jesus visits us, comforts us and bestows upon us His miracles.

Through the Holy Spirit, Jesus also restored Peter. After Jesus' resurrection, Peter and the other disciples collapsed again. But after they were baptized with the Holy Spirit on the day of Pentecost in Mark's upper room, Peter and all the disciples were completely changed and filled with the power of the Holy Spirit. Peter especially completely threw off the sense of failure and despair and became a servant of God, boldly witnessing to Jesus' death and resurrection. Baptized in the Holy Spirit, Peter became such a powerful witness for Jesus that 3,000 people were converted through a single sermon (Acts 2:41). Also, he became a miracle-working man, even raising a cripple to wholeness through the power of Christ in his life (Acts 3:1-10).

Any Christian who has met Jesus Christ as his personal Saviour may fall into temptation and despair if he takes off the helmet of faith and looks to his own resources. But Jesus comes today to visit us all, the fallen and the weak. Through the Holy Spirit, He wants to meet us today just as He met Peter. Just as Peter became a miracle-producing servant of God after receiving the baptism of the Holy Spirit, we, too, can become a miracle-producing servant after we have been filled with the Holy Spirit. Let us be baptized in the Holy Spirit and live a victorious life in the fullness of the Holy Spirit!

CLOSING QUESTIONS

> ### What did Peter say when Jesus told the disciples that he must die?
> (Matthew 16:22)

> ### What did Jesus say mattered more to Peter than God's work?
> (Matthew 16:23)

> ### When Jesus appeared the third time to his disciples, what did He invite them to do?
> (John 21:12)

APPLICATION

1. Let Peter's confession be our confession: *"You are the Christ, the Son of the living God."*

2. After receiving the baptism of the Holy Spirit, Peter was completely delivered from his old passiveness. He became a new man, a miracle-working servant of God for His glory. Let us pray for the fullness of the Holy Spirit and live a life of miracles in the Lord Jesus Christ.

JESUS ON THE MOUNT OF
TRANSFIGURATION

1. **Today's Scripture**
   Matthew 17:1-13
2. **Memory Verse**
   Matthew 17:5
   While Peter was talking, a bright cloud covered them. A voice came from the cloud. The voice said "This is my son and I love him. I am very pleased with him. Obey him!"
3. **Reference Scripture**
   Isaiah 42:1
   Luke 9:28-36
4. **Objectives**
   a. Let us realize that our body will be transformed like Jesus' glorious body when we meet Him in the clouds.
   b. Let us recognize that Jesus is the One Who fulfilled the law and prophecies, and He is never to be compared with Moses, who represents the law nor Elijah, who represents the prophets.
   c. Let us all become like sheep that recognize Jesus' voice calling us.

LEADING QUESTIONS

> **What was Jesus' appearance like when He was transfigured before His three loving disciples?**
> (Matthew 17:2)

> **Whom was the transfigured Jesus talking with?**
> (Matthew 17:3)

> **After they gained their composure and lifted up their faces, who did the three disciples see on the mountain?**
> (Matthew 17:8)

TODAY'S MESSAGE

Jesus once took His beloved disciples, Peter, James and John to a high mountain and He was transfigured before them. His face shone like the sun, and his clothes became as white as the light. Then Moses and Elijah appeared and talked with Him.

Jesus Alone

The disciples of Jesus could not help but be aghast at the awesome scene. Peter, who was acting like the spokesman for the three, bravely opened his mouth:

"Lord, it is good that we are here. If you want, I will put three tents here – one for you, one for Moses and one for Elijah."

Actually, in his bewilderment, Peter did not know what he was talking about. Immediately a cloud overshadowed them and a voice spoke:

"This is my Son and I love him. I am very pleased with him. Obey him!"

The disciples fell on their faces and trembled but Jesus touched them, saying:

"Stand up. Don't be afraid."

When they turned around they found only Jesus was there.

The Tabernacle of Jesus Christ

The above scene teaches us several things.

First, when Jesus was transfigured and clothed in a glorious light on the mountain, Moses and Elijah appeared and spoke with Jesus. Moses and Elijah are two representatives of God in the Old Testament and both were witnesses of the glory of Christ.

Moses, as the representative of the law, witnessed about Christ through laws and sacrificial rituals. Elijah, as the representative of the prophets who followed the period of the law, witnessed about salvation and Christ Who was to come.

The magnificent glory of the transfigured Jesus is the glory that the law and the prophets of the Old Testament witnessed about. As written in the law and the prophets, when Christ came in the flesh for the work of redemption, Moses and Elijah as witnesses of the Old Testament appeared before the disciples.

Second, Peter spoke erroneous words. Peter unwittingly suggested to Jesus that they should build three tents or tabernacles (AV), one for Jesus, one for Moses and one for Elijah. This was a grave mistake. Because Moses and Elijah were only witnesses of Jesus' glory and they were merely on an errand, they should never have been placed equal with Jesus. The laws and prophecies were to be fulfilled and accomplished in Christ and they were never meant to stand side by side with Jesus.

Third, God corrected Peter's error. When Peter began to place the law and the prophets equally with Jesus, God spoke from the glory of the cloud and corrected Peter by saying:

> "This is my Son and I love him. I am very pleased with him. Obey him!"

The disciples then looked round and found that Moses and Elijah had been taken up to heaven by God.

The law and the prophets were meant only to witness that Jesus is the sole Saviour of man and their witnessing had already been completed in Jesus. This teaches us that our only Saviour, who deserves our worship and trust, is Jesus Christ.

According to God's command, we should not build a tabernacle to anyone but Jesus. Likewise, the laws, prophecies, denominations, theologies, all these are merely for witnessing to the glory of Jesus, thus they should never stand on the same level with Jesus.

The Meaning of Jesus' Transfiguration

Then what does this transfiguration incident mean to us?

First, this is foretelling that our mortal body will also be transformed in the not-too-distant future, just as Jesus' glorious body was (Philippians 3:21). So we must earnestly look for and expect Jesus' return to earth as the King of kings. As those disciples climbed hard to follow Jesus to the mountain, we should also remember that after our brief moment of hardship on earth we will be given the privilege of enjoying God's glory.

Second, Jesus talked with Moses and Elijah. It is described in detail in Luke 9:30-31. They were talking about Jesus' crucifixion, which is evidence that our blessing of transfiguration, like Jesus' glorious body, is possible because Jesus was crucified on the cross.

Third, there was a voice from God: *"Obey him!"* This voice of our Father in heaven still commands us today to listen to Jesus. Jesus came to us as our Shepherd Who gives us life and abundant blessings. When we hear His voice, we can receive abundant food from Him. We also have an obligation to please our heavenly Father, by growing in faith. Faith comes when we hear God's Word.

Before we take or receive any human philosophy or knowledge by which to live, we must take the Word of God first, love His Word and experience his Word in our lives through miracles.

CLOSING QUESTIONS

> ### When was Jesus transfigured?
> (Luke 9:29)

> ### We are Jesus' sheep.
> ### Whose voice do we have to hear?
> (John 10:3)

> ### How will our mortal body be transformed by Jesus?
> (Philippians 3:21)

APPLICATION

1. When Jesus returns we will be transformed, to have a glorious body like His. Therefore, let us keep ourselves holy in thought and deed, looking forward with great expectation to His Second Coming!

2. Jesus is God, so He could never be compared with Moses or Elijah. Therefore we must always give Jesus the first place in our lives.

JESUS' ENTRANCE INTO
JERUSALEM

1. **Today's Scripture**
   Matthew 21:1-11
2. **Memory Verse**
   Matthew 21:9
   Some of the people were walking ahead of Jesus. Others were walking behind him. All the people were shouting, "Praise to the Son of David! God bless the One who comes in the name of the Lord! Praise to God in heaven!"
3. **Reference Scripture**
   Zechariah 9:9
   Luke 19:29-44
4. **Objectives**
   a. As Jesus portrayed a humble and peaceable attitude when He entered Jerusalem on a donkey, let us become believers who are examples of humility and peace to others.
   b. Let us become believers who return praise and glory to Jesus.
   c. Let us become believers who will meet Jesus returning as the King of kings, and as our bridegroom.

LEADING QUESTIONS

> **On what did Jesus ride as He entered Jerusalem?**
> (Matthew 21:1-7)

> **What does this indicate about Jesus' character?**
> (Matthew 21:5)

> **What was the response of the people as Jesus came into Jerusalem?**
> (Matthew 21:10)

TODAY'S MESSAGE

A few days before Jesus suffered on the cross, He entered the city of Jerusalem receiving praise and glory. His entering into Jerusalem was not just a simple passing event. In this lesson we will study three points of significance in His entrance into Jerusalem.

The Donkey-Riding Jesus

On His way to Jerusalem, Jesus arrived at Bethphage, near the Mount of Olives and He sent two disciples to the village to bring a donkey and its colt. Jesus told them that if anyone asked anything, just to answer, *"The Master needs them."*

So Jesus entered the city of Jerusalem on the donkey His disciples brought to Him. A great crowd who followed Jesus spread their garments on the road for Him and also cut down branches from the trees, spreading them on the road, crying out with praises to Jesus:
> *"Praise to the Son of David! God bless the One who comes in the name of the Lord! Praise to God in heaven!"*

We can find a few astonishing facts in this scene.

The first fact is that Jesus' riding on a donkey was foretold in the scriptures. About five hundred years before Jesus was born, the prophet Zechariah spoke:
> *"Your King is coming to you. He is gentle and riding on a donkey. He is on the colt of a donkey."* (Matthew 21:5)

And to fulfil the word spoken through the prophet, He really rode on a donkey. Jesus, as the Son of God, could have entered Jerusalem in a most pompous manner but to fulfil the Word of God, Jesus humbled Himself and rode on a donkey.

With humility like this, Jesus not only rode on a donkey to enter Jerusalem, but was obedient to the death on a cross to save us, according to His Father's will (Matthew 26:39, 42).

Jesus' riding on a donkey showed His humility. He could have entered the city with a host of angels mobilized and with the great sound of a trumpet, but He came *".... gentle and riding on a donkey"* (Zechariah 9:9, Matthew 21:5). Before this entrance to Jerusalem, to disciples and people, He spoke about Himself:
> *"I am gentle and humble in spirit."* (Matthew 11:29)

As shown above, Jesus' words and deeds were completely different from those of the Pharisees and scribes. Today, we, as Jesus' believers and followers, should be lowly before God and people as Jesus has taught us.

The Praise-Receiving Jesus

When Jesus was entering Jerusalem, a great crowd cried, shouting: *"Praise to God in Heaven!"* In the Authorized Version their cry reads *"Hosanna in the highest!"* Hosanna means "save or help us now". At that time, Israel was occupied by the Roman Empire. The people of Israel were oppressed and exploited like slaves by the Roman government. Because Jesus appeared and performed miracles under such circumstances, the Israelites thought Jesus would be their deliverer who would save them from the Roman Empire. In other words, the Jewish people misunderstood the purpose of Jesus' coming to earth. He came to give life and freedom to all mankind, who were under the curse of death in the captivity of Satan's bondage, resulting from Adam and Eve's fall. Jesus came to revive our dead souls by His precious blood shed on the cross, so that we would be given the threefold blessings of salvation from Him:

"Beloved, I wish above all things that thou mayest prosper and be in health, even as thy soul prospereth." (3 John 2 AV)

Now the Israelites were greatly disappointed that Jesus would not be their deliverer from the Roman Empire. But Jesus did not change His way. He was destined to bear the cross according to the plan of God so that the price of man's sin would be paid. Soon enough, the praise of Hosanna from the lips of the Jews disappeared and they began to shout: "Crucify Him on the cross."

The children continued praising Jesus, *"Praise to the son of David"* but the high priests, Pharisees and scribes became indignant towards them. Jesus rebuked the wicked leaders:

"I tell you, if my followers don't say these things, then the stones will cry out." (Luke 19:40)

He quoted a scripture from Old Testament prophecy:

"You have taught children and babies to sing praises." (Matthew 21:16)

The love of God and the redeeming work of Jesus Christ was so great that even stones could not keep silent but would praise Him. Today, we too should live a life of praising Jesus with pure hearts as children.

Jesus, the King of Kings

When Jesus entered Jerusalem, people spread their garments on His pathway and shouted, *"God bless the King of Israel!"* (John 12:13)

What kind of a king was He? He did not use a horse, but a donkey. A horse is a symbol of war, while a donkey is a peace symbol. Jesus came to earth as the King of peace, to give us peace. When He was born, angelic hosts also witnessed that He is the King of peace:

"Give glory to God in heaven, and on earth let there be peace to the people who please God." (Luke 2:14)

One clear piece of evidence that Jesus came as a king is shown in the fact that the people spread their garments on the road for Him. We can see in 2 Kings 9:13 that people put their garments before Jehu when he was made king. The spreading of people's garments before Jesus' pathway tells us that Jesus entered the city indeed as our king.

However, Jesus' kingdom does not belong to this world; it is the kingdom of heaven. It is the kingdom of God that the returning Jesus will rule. Through Jesus Christ we became citizens of the kingdom of God and Jesus became our king and ruler. When Jesus cleansed the temple with a king's authority, no one there defied Jesus. In the very near future Jesus will return to earth as the King of kings. Everyday we should praise Jesus, our King of peace, and live in hope and joy expecting His return.

CLOSING QUESTIONS

To whom does God give His grace?
(1 Peter 5:5)

What is better than sacrifice?
(1 Samuel 15:22)

When Jesus rode on a donkey, what was fulfilled?
(Matthew 21:4)

APPLICATION

1. God wants more of our obedience than our sacrifice. Let us obey God's Word and live under His abundant blessing.

2. Following Jesus' example for true humility, let us live a truly humble life through our words and deeds.

3. Let us live with the dignity that we are God-reckoned kingly priests.

JESUS' ANOINTING FOR BURIAL

1. **Today's Scripture**
   Mark 14:1-9 (Read both AV and EB versions.)
2. **Memory Verse**
   Mark 14:8 (EB)
   "This women did the only thing she could for me. She poured perfume on my body. She did this before I die to prepare me for burial."
3. **Reference Scripture**
   Matthew 26:6-13
   John 12:2-8
4. **Objectives**
   a. As Mary broke open her precious box of ointment for Jesus (Mark 14:3 AV), let us allow ourselves to be broken so that we may live God-centred lives instead of self-centred lives.
   b. Breaking "self" means sowing our faith deeper in God. Let us live every day sowing our faith deeper and deeper.
   c. Throughout our life, let us partake in Jesus' suffering and death.

LEADING QUESTIONS

> **How much was Mary's ointment-perfume worth?**
> (Mark 14:3-5)

> **Who was one of those who rebuked Mary's deed?**
> (John 12:4-6)

> **What did Jesus say about Mary's action?**
> (Mark 14:6-9)

TODAY'S MESSAGE

Jesus is indeed pleased when we offer Him what we cherish most. Through the story of Mary breaking open her most precious alabaster box for the sake of Jesus' burial, we will study the faith that leads us to break ourselves. The more precious our faith becomes to us, the more we desire to be broken before God, until we make the moves necessary to allow ourselves to be broken.

Mary and Judas Iscariot

One week before He was nailed to the cross, Jesus was invited for a meal by Simon in the town of Bethany. Simon was a leper. By sharing a meal with lepers, who were despised by all people in those days, Jesus showed His love to those who were outcasts.

Jesus and His disciples were there when Mary brought her precious perfume that she had been saving carefully for her marriage. She broke open the box and poured the perfume on Jesus' head. To Mary, expressing her gratitude to Jesus mattered more than her carefully made plans for marriage, so she could boldly sacrifice her dowry for His sake. Though she was giving up her cherished ointment-perfume, a fountain of joy was overflowing from her heart.

In the same room, at the same hour, was Judas Iscariot. When he saw what Mary was doing for the Lord Jesus, he became furious and made an outburst:

> *"This perfume was worth 300 silver coins. It should have been sold and the money given to the poor."* (John 12:5)

He seemed to act out of charity, but he was really acting for selfish reasons because he was a thief (John 12:6). In fact Judas never loved Jesus. Judas followed Jesus only out of political ambition. Because he found Jesus always talking about the kingdom of heaven instead of the political kingdom on earth, Judas became greatly disappointed, and he eventually sold Jesus for 30 pieces of silver.

The Alabaster Box that Mary Broke Open

Mary's breaking open of her alabaster box was more than just an ordinary sacrifice. In those days, it was a Jewish custom for maidens to bring their alabaster box containing this precious perfume to their bridegroom's home. The more perfume they had, the better they were treated by the husband's household. Thus, Jewish daughters and their parents did their utmost to save as much precious perfume for the marriage as they could.

Mary, being fatherless and motherless, probably earned the perfume all by herself. It was said to be worth 300 silver coins, or denarii, an amount equal to a labourer's wage for 300 days. It was so precious that she spent her life saving it and putting it aside.

When Jesus visited Bethany, Mary was determined to show her affection and gratitude to Jesus through this unusual deed. With a heart for serving Him unreservedly, giving up her lifetime's saving did not seem like a loss, so she willingly broke open her expensive box. Pouring the fragrant perfume over Jesus' head and feet, she knelt down and humbly washed His feet with her long hair. That was His anointing for burial, as He was to go to the cross one week later.

By giving her saving of a lifetime dowry to Jesus, Mary in fact offered her past, and her future too, at the feet of her Lord. Her deed glorified Jesus and He blessed her, saying that wherever the Good News was preached, what she had done would be told and people would remember her (Mark 14:9).

The supreme proof of our faith in our Heavenly Father is in breaking open our "box" – our life – for the Lord Jesus by mortifying our "self". Many people break their lives in a quest for money, fame, power or pleasure on earth. But life is like withering grass or a flower which will fade away only too soon. Only the Word of God exists eternally.

Our Lord Jesus broke His body for us. Therefore we too should allow ourselves to be broken to prove our determination that we will dedicate ourselves to the Lord Jesus under any circumstances. When we do so, the aroma of our faith will ascend to heaven as a sweet-smelling sacrifice and the Lord will be pleased to receive it.

The Breaking Process

Then what must we do to break ourselves? Our egotistic nature is not easily broken. This breaking process is only possible when we allow the Lord God to do it. Then He does do it.

First, he breaks us through His Word. When we hear or read God's Word, the "self" which belongs to the flesh is broken and our egotistic nature is peeled off, little by little.

Second, we may be broken through the blessing of the Holy Spirit. When we recognize the Holy Spirit, welcome Him and love Him, He begins to break us and open our spiritual eyes little by little, more and more, so that He can guide us to the realm of God's providence.

Our Lord also breaks us through suffering. By allowing us to go through various hardships of life, He makes our ego surrender to Him and the purpose He has in mind for us. When we come forward to the Lord, surrendering with our hands up, the Holy Spirit takes over, occupies us and begins His breaking process.

When the Holy Spirit touched Mary, she could willingly break open her box of precious perfume because of her deep affection and gratitude to Jesus. She had also gone through a dark valley of her life when her bother Lazarus died, but during her sorrow she had really tasted Jesus' love and power and she could give up what she cared for the most. When one trusts in Jesus, there is evidence of brokenness in that life. People in this world want sinful things and are too proud of what they have, but as believers we live a Jesus life through breaking open our life "boxes". Whether it be death or life we belong to Jesus. And our Lord Jesus is preparing an eternal new heaven and new Jerusalem for all of us.

CLOSING QUESTIONS

> ### How does the book of Hebrews describe the breaking of our souls?
> (Hebrews 4:12)

> ### What is God's purpose in calling us?
> a. Romans 8:29
> b. Ephesians 1:4
> c. 1 Peter 2:9

> ### What are the things that God demands from us?
> a. Proverbs 27:2
> b. Micah 6:8
> c. Romans 12:3

APPLICATION

1. What is our "box" that can be broken open before the Lord? Ask yourself if it has been broken or not before Jesus.

2. For our precious lives to be broken, we must "eat" the Word, develop a prayer life and also give thanks to Jesus even under trials. When we do so, we will know the blessing and humility that comes from being broken.

JESUS WASHES HIS DISCIPLES' FEET

1. **Today's Scripture**
   John 13:1-17
2. **Memory Verse**
   John 13:10
   Jesus said, "After a person has had a bath, his whole body is clean. He needs only to wash his feet. And you men are clean, but not all of you."
3. **Reference Scripture**
   Matthew 20:20-28
4. **Objectives**
   a. Let us understand that Jesus loves us even unto death. He does not condemn us nor curse us.
   b. By following Jesus' example of lowly service to man, let us become believers with humility and a servant-heart.

LEADING QUESTIONS

> **Peter said "No! You will never wash my feet."**
> **What did Jesus answer?**
> (John 13:6-8)

> **What part of the body did Jesus say needed to be washed even if one had already been bathed?**
> (John 13:10)

> **What was the purpose of Jesus washing His disciples' feet?**
> (John 13:14-15)

TODAY'S MESSAGE

The night before the feast of the Passover and His crucifixion, Jesus washed the feet of His disciples in John Mark's upper room. Jesus taught the disciples to wash each other's feet as He had washed their feet. Through the lowly task of washing His disciples' feet, we will learn about Jesus' love, humility and life of service. We will also study the way our sins are cleansed.

Jesus' Unending Love

The purpose of Jesus' coming to this earth was to bear man's sin on the cross and expand the kingdom of heaven, but His disciples thought Jesus would become the King of Israel and demolish the Roman government. They even quarrelled over who would have the highest position when Jesus was inaugurated as king.

To correct the wrong motives and actions of His disciples, Jesus washed their feet. One noticeable thing here is that Jesus' expression of complete humility and love was shown the very night before He hung on the cross. In other words before He left this earth, Jesus showed us an example of humility as the most important teaching for His followers. In essence, He was saying, "If I have condescended to do this for you, then you should be willing to do this lowest service for each other."

Jesus manifested humility as His expression of affection for people. The most beautiful fruit of love is humility and willing service for others. Jesus lowered Himself and
> gave up his place with God and made himself nothing. He was
> born to be a man and became like a servant

because He loved the Father (Philippians 2:7). He also manifested His unending love for us by humbling Himself and dying on the cross.

Jesus' Ministry

The land of Palestine where Jesus lived is mostly dry and sandy. People's footwear was like today's sandals so their feet were naturally very dirty after a short journey. It was the custom for every household to keep a water jar at the entrance, and whenever guests arrived the servant of the house would wash their feet. However, Jesus' disciples were preoccupied with the strife concerning who would move up to higher positions when Jesus was made king, so they apparently did not even bother to wash each other's feet (Luke 22:24).

Then Jesus took off His robe, picked up a towel and began to wash His disciples' feet. The hand of the very Son of God, the Messiah, began to wash those smelly and filthy feet. At first, they were perplexed and probably stared at each other. Soon enough they began to understand what He was doing and why. Then they probably blushed and fell on their faces with shame. There are three important lessons in today's scriptures:

First, Jesus showed us an example of humility. Girding Himself with a towel and washing their feet was a true manifestation of his humility (1 Peter 5:5). By washing His own disciples' feet, Jesus humbled Himself to the lowest position, that of a true servant.

Second, Jesus, in washing their feet, showed His purpose for coming to earth.

> "In the same way, the Son of Man did not come to be served. He came to serve. The Son of Man came to give his life to save many people." (Mark 10:45)

Third, Jesus provided an example for the disciples' daily lives. He confirmed this in John 13:14-15:

> "I, your Lord and Teacher, have washed your feet: So you also should wash each other's feet. I did this as an example for you. So you should do as I have done for you."

Believing in Jesus and following Him means a life of ministering to our neighbours and others just as Jesus did. It means worshipping the Lord by helping others, no matter how lowly the need, and still respecting them. This life of serving others is possible only when we esteem other people better than ourselves.

Jesus Taught Repentance

In washing their feet, Jesus was also teaching the disciples about repentance and being born again. When Jesus turned to wash Peter's feet, he tried to stop the Lord:

> "No! You will never wash my feet."

Jesus rebuked him:

> "If I don't wash your feet, then you are not one of my people."

Peter spoke again:

> "Lord, after you wash my feet, wash my hands and my head too."

The Lord answered again:

> After a person has had a bath, his whole body is clean. He needs only to wash his feet." (John 13:10)

Why did Jesus make a distinction between "have a bath" and "only wash his feet?" By the words "have a bath", Jesus meant a sinner who is already totally washed, a born-again believer.

Man is born once into the world. Only by repenting of his sins and accepting Jesus into his heart, can he be spiritually born of God, become His child and be saved. This is the rebirth known as being "born again".

Once a person has been "born again", the Holy Spirit has entered his life and does not depart. If he sins, sins will change his relationship and he must repent again and be cleansed by the precious blood of Jesus, but the Holy Spirit will patiently remain and deal with him in many ways to bring him to repentance again and restore him to full fellowship with Jesus. That was what Jesus meant, when he said that a person who has had a bath does not need to be bathed again, but need only wash his feet.

Then what did Jesus mean by "washing only feet"? Though we are born again, our "feet" are like our faith. Our faith is easily defiled because we are influenced by our environment. Just as we wash our feet again often, we must also repent often of the sins which we have committed consciously or unconsciously, so that we keep ourselves clean before the Lord. This is what Jesus meant.

Through this lesson in washing our feet, Jesus taught us the way to deal with those sins, large or small, that beset believers from time to time, so that He can bestow upon us abundant blessings, miracles and answered prayers. We should daily seek the help of the Holy Spirit to live a life of cleansing, sanctifying ourselves and ministering to others.

CLOSING QUESTIONS

> **What was the purpose of Jesus' coming to earth?**
> (Mark 10:45)

> **How did Jesus say a person could become great?**
> (Mark 10:43-44)

> **What was Jesus' purpose in giving us His example of suffering wrongfully?**
> (1 Peter 2:21)

Now consider the application of this lesson which you will find on the next page.

APPLICATION

1. Jesus loved us unto death, so let us always thank Him for our eternal life.

2. Let us minister to others with that same kind of love.

3. When we fail and commit sins because of weaknesses in our lives, let us quickly repent, and cleanse our hearts so that we will never break fellowship with Him but have His blessings continually.

JESUS ESTABLISHES
COMMUNION

1. **Today's Scripture**
   Matthew 26:17-29
2. **Memory Verse**
   Matthew 26:28
   "This is my blood which begins the new agreement that God makes with his people. This blood is poured out for many to forgive their sins."
3. **Reference Scripture**
   Mark 14:22-25
   1 Corinthians 11:23-26
4. **Objectives**
   a. Day by day let us draw even closer to the Word of God and live there.
   b. Let us remind ourselves that there is total healing in the communion, as well as wholesome health of our spirit, soul and body, if we discern the Lord's body during communion.

LEADING QUESTIONS

> ### Where did the Lord's supper take place?
> (Matthew 26:18-19)

> ### What did Jesus say the bread and wine represented, respectively?
> (Matthew 26:26-28)

> ### When will Jesus partake of the Lord's supper again?
> (Matthew 26:29)

TODAY'S MESSAGE

Before he died, Jesus shared the Passover supper with His disciples. This was the origin of our communion service as we know it today. Jesus declared the bread represented His flesh which was torn and the wine represented His blood which was shed for our sake. This was foretold through the Passover lamb's body and blood when the Israelite people escaped from the land of Egypt 1400 years previously.

Jesus came to earth to become spiritual manna or "food" for us. This lesson will teach us how Jesus' flesh and blood have become our food.

Jesus is Food for our Spirit

Because of Adam and Eve's sin, the spirit of man died. Man's fellowship with God was severed and man's physical body was to die eventually and to go to the lake of fire and brimstone.

To quicken the dead state of man, God's only begotten Son, Jesus Christ, came to earth clothed in flesh and shed His blood. His crucifixion and resurrection became the power of life to quicken our dead spirits, because He paid the debt of our sins that we should have paid ourselves.

Now that the debt has been paid, when we reach out to Jesus the Holy Spirit enters our lives and we receive eternal life. Through eating His flesh and drinking His blood at the communion table we are able to have new spiritual fellowship with God.

Jesus is food for our spirit. Every day we must "eat" of Him. In this world of wilderness He is our spiritual manna. We must welcome Him, rely on Him and feed on His Word regularly so that the inner man will be renewed daily. When we do so, His life will overflow in us, so that we can live victoriously with a faith and power in our hearts that people of the world do not know of.

Jesus is Food for our Mind

The communion, which represents the flesh and blood of Jesus, is food for the minds of believers, too. The human mind consists of intellect, emotions and will. Natural men of the world live by the power of their intellect, exercised through their senses. But we believers strive to live by divine wisdom, which is revelation knowledge from above, and God consistently gives us revelation knowledge as we eat of His Word.

Through the revelation knowledge from above, our outlook on the world and our perspectives on our life, society and history, become entirely different from the views of unbelievers. We know that God created the heavens and earth, and we are His creatures so we should therefore live according to His commandments and all of His Word. We also view human history as God's sovereign, providential and redemptive plan for mankind. As to death, we have a view that earthly death is just a passageway to heaven for us.

By believing in Jesus, He also becomes a great food for our emotions. Destructive feelings such as hatred, fear, frustration, anger, jealousy and envy in our hearts will be changed to the love, hope and faith of Jesus. Joy and mercy will also spring from our hearts.

Jesus' flesh and blood also become food for our will. Before we believed in Jesus, we were motivated by selfishness and we could not control our intellect, emotions and will to obey God's will. We were simply not capable of overcoming our corrupt and licentious mind. But when we eat of Jesus' body, His life flows through us and we are enabled to control our will daily so that we gradually become God-centred instead of self-centred, and concerned for others instead of only for ourselves.

So Jesus Christ becomes food for our intellect, emotions and will. I urge you to reach out to Jesus anew as you partake of the communion cup and receive whatever you need from all of His provision.

Jesus Christ is Food for our Body

God cursed the ground when Adam and Eve sinned:
> "I will put a curse on the ground. You will have to work very hard for food. In pain you will eat its food all the days of your life. The ground will produce thorns and weeds for you ...."
> (Genesis 3:17-18)

But as Jesus took our sins at Calvary, our curse was removed. The Bible records:
> So the law put a curse on us, but Christ took away that curse. He changed places with us and put himself under that curse. It is written in the Scriptures:
> "Everyone whose body is displayed on a tree is cursed."
> (Galations 3:13)

Because Jesus became our curse, we have been redeemed from every curse. When we partake of the symbols of His broken body and shed blood at the Lord's table, we will experience the bondage of the curse, thorns and thistles departing from us and we will enter into the blessings of Abraham. Those who partake of the symbols of Jesus' flesh and blood are indeed blessed.

Jesus also takes our sicknesses and with His healing power He keeps us well while we live in this world. He bore our infirmity and sickness so that we would be able to live a healthy life. Jesus is truly spiritual manna for our health.

When we partake of the communion, we must remember that before He was crucified, Jesus took bread and when He had given thanks He instructed His disciples to take it and eat. Then He ordained that we believers must do this often in remembrance of Him also. It is because the communion cup represents all we will need for spirit, soul and body. Also, we must share this good news with others so that they too can be healthy, strong Christians in body, soul and spirit by partaking of the communion.

CLOSING QUESTIONS

> ### To what did Jesus liken Himself?
> (John 6:35)

> ### What is the purpose of partaking of communion?
> (1 Corinthians 11:24-26)

> ### What should our attitude be before communion?
> (1 Corinthians 11:28)

APPLICATION

1. Partaking of communion is a mandate as well as a privilege for believers. Let us always take time to prepare our hearts before receiving the symbols of His broken body, so that we will always receive exactly what we need from the Lord and be blessed greatly.

2. True communion is actually meeting with God and having fellowship with our Christian brethren. Through communion, let us establish or re-establish the correct relationship with God and our fellow Christians, so that we may be strong physically and spiritually.

JESUS'
SUFFERING

1. **Today's Scripture**
   Matthew 26:36-75
2. **Memory Verse**
   Matthew 26:67
   Then the people there spit in Jesus' face and beat him with their fists. Others slapped Jesus.
3. **Reference Scripture**
   Mark 14:43-52
   Luke 22:47-53
4. **Objectives**
   a. By reflecting on Jesus' life of suffering, let us thank Him for His suffering for us.
   b. Jesus could have avoided the suffering, but out of obedience He willingly took the cross. Let us follow the example of Jesus' love and total submission to our Father.
   c. By understanding clearly the meaning of Jesus' suffering, let us partake in His suffering with a glad heart too.

LEADING QUESTIONS

> **Whose will did Jesus always want to follow?**
> (Matthew 26:39)

> **What did the chief priest, elders and all the council try to find in order to have a reason to put Jesus to death?**
> (Matthew 26:59)

> **What kind of mock accusations did Jesus receive at the court of the high priest?**
> (Matthew 26:65-67)

TODAY'S MESSAGE

During the Passover feast, Jesus washed His disciples' feet in John Mark's upper room and there He instituted the Lord's Supper. He prayed with a heavy heart and tears in the

267

garden of Gethsemane, as He prepared for His destination, the cross. As truly God and truly man, He lived a life of suffering during his 33 years on earth.

Through this lesson, we will learn the true meaning of Jesus' suffering and what our attitude should be to the suffering in our lives.

Jesus' Life of Suffering

Jesus' life was full of sufferings from the very beginning. When He left His heavenly throne and became man, He began to know suffering. Being sought out by Herod and having to escape to Egypt immediately after His birth was an experience of suffering. Being both God and man, He lived on earth as we do, for thirty years experiencing hunger, tiredness and being misunderstood. As soon as He began His public ministry, He was led to a wilderness for forty days of fasting and was tempted by the devil. Though He was sent by God, He was rejected by the scribes and Pharisees.

In the garden of Gethsemane, the sweat and blood He shed during intense prayer for us was a suffering that was beyond description.

On the eve of His crucifixion, He was questioned by the high priests, King Herod and Pontius Pilate. He was mocked and spat on by the very people He was going to save. They cried out: "Crucify him, crucify him."

Soldiers scourged Him with whips bearing iron nails and, mocking Him further, they cast lots for His garment. Some soldiers, after spitting on Jesus, struck Him demanding: "Prophesy to us, Christ!"

The same night the Passover lamb was slain, Jesus was hung on the cross as God's sacrificial lamb, taking the sins of the world. Jesus, Who came to pay the penalty for man's sin, lived a life of suffering both physical and mental, which reached its peak on the cross. Isaiah 52:14 adds further:
> "His appearance was so changed he did not look like a man.
> His form was changed so much they could barely tell he was
> human."

Yes, Jesus knew what it was to suffer.

Jesus Could Have Avoided His Suffering

Could Jesus have avoided this kind of shame and suffering on the cross? Yes. There were several occasions when He could have avoided the suffering before He was nailed on the cross, if He had chosen to do so.

The first occasion was when Jesus climbed the Mount of Transfiguration (Luke 9:28). While He was praying there, His countenance suddenly changed and Moses and Elijah appeared. Together they talked about Jesus' crucifixion which was to take place in Jerusalem soon. If Jesus had refused to go to the cross, in order to avoid the suffering and pain, He could have returned to His Father when the cloud overshadowed Him as He spoke with Moses and Elijah. But when the clouds cleared away Jesus was still there alone. He had determined not to avoid the purpose of the cross even though it meant suffering.

Second, Jesus could have escaped in Jerusalem when He came to prepare the Passover feast. A few Greek people had gathered there and had extended an invitation to Jesus to visit their country. If Jesus had chosen to he could have gone with them and lived comfortably, receiving respect and glory, but He chose to take the cross.

In Gethsemane also, Jesus could have escaped when the soldiers came to arrest Him. Nervous Peter cut off the ear of a high priest's servant with His sword but Jesus put it back on and healed it, declaring to Peter:

"Surely you know I could ask my Father, and he would give me more than 12 armies of angels?"

Jesus was not arrested because of His powerlessness. Remember, He could have left this earth at the Mount of Transfiguration, or He could have gone to Greece. But instead of choosing His own way, He chose the way of obedience which included suffering. He wanted to save us through the plan of the cross because there was no other plan for our redemption.

Our Attitude Towards Suffering

What truth is Jesus teaching us here about suffering? Without exception everyone in this life experiences suffering, whether it is a little or much.

Some are crushed or shipwrecked by hardships, while others obtain glory and victory when they come through such difficulties. What makes the difference? Does the suffering itself cause shipwreck or victory? No. Suffering itself does not have the power nor the right to make us fail or succeed. The answer is in our *attitude* towards the suffering.

First, there are people who always have a negative attitude when they encounter problems. When difficulties come, they always grumble about their circumstances and blame others for their problems. As a result, they allow their hardships to crush them.

But other people take a different attitude towards hardships. When sorrow and painful suffering attacks, they take an attitude of faith that somehow God will bring a blessing out of the trouble. With faith in their hearts they advance to a richer and more blessed life.

Scripture tells us the Apostle Paul had a painful problem but he steadfastly trusted the Lord Jesus and finally confessed:

So I am happy when I have weaknesses, insults, hard times, sufferings and all kinds of troubles. All these are for Christ. And I am happy, because when I am weak, then I am truly strong. (2 Corinthians 12:10)

He overcame his difficulty and still became a great apostle to proclaim the good news to the world.

When we take a positive attitude in the Lord Jesus and overcome our suffering we will become stronger too.

One thing we should distinguish is that the only suffering that can be labelled persecution is that which we suffer for the sake of Jesus and the spreading of His gospel. Except for such persecution, hardships from lack of food, shelter or clothing should not be labelled as "persecution" by believers, because Jesus Christ redeemed us from the spiritual, physical and circumstantial curse. Enduring hardships for the sake of preaching the gospel in order to destroy Satan's work can be labelled partaking in the suffering of Jesus. These sufferings will be greatly rewarded some day when we see Jesus (Matthew 5:11,12).

CLOSING QUESTIONS

> **The Psalmist confessed that being afflicted was good for him. What benefit can we receive from affliction?**
> (Psalm 119:71)

> **Why are we able to rejoice when we partake of Christ's sufferings?**
> (1 Peter 4:13)

> **What lesson does Jesus' suffering teach us?**
> (Hebrews 2:18, 12:3)

APPLICATION

1. Let us always remember the redemptive suffering of Jesus was in our stead. Let us live always with thanksgiving to Him.

2. When hardships come, let us draw strength and overcoming power from the Lord through our faith. Let us remember every test or trial that we face has passed through our Father's loving hands with His approval, and that He enables us to come through victoriously!

JESUS
DIES FOR US

1. **Today's Scripture**
   Matthew 27:11-56
2. **Memory Verse**
   Matthew 27:46
   And about three o'clock Jesus cried out in a loud voice, "Eli, Eli, lema sabachthani?" This means, "My God, my God, why have you left me alone?"
3. **Reference Scripture**
   Isaiah 53:4-7
4. **Objectives**
   a. Let us ever give thanks and praise to Jesus Who died on the cross to redeem us from sins.
   b. Let us enjoy the total blessings of salvation: spiritually, circumstantially, physically.
   c. Let us mortify our fleshly lust and sins on the cross every day.

LEADING QUESTIONS

> ### What did the Jewish people request Pilate to do with Jesus?
> (Matthew 27:22-25)

> ### Where was Jesus hung on the cross?
> (Matthew 27:33)

> ### What sign of accusation was placed above His head on the cross?
> (Matthew 27:37)

TODAY'S MESSAGE

The suffering of Jesus climaxed with His death. He did not turn away from the bitter cup but drank it and endured the cross and its torment until salvation's debt was paid. High priests and scribes mocked Him saying He saved others but He could not save Himself. Why should Jesus, the God-Man, have allowed His life to end so tragically? We will review these reasons and the awesome meaning and power of His death.

273

To Fulfil the Father's Will

The reason Jesus did not come down from the cross was to fulfil the
Word of God. It prophesied in Genesis 3:15:
> *"I will make you and the woman enemies to each other. Your
> descendants and her descendants will be enemies. Her child
> will crush your head. And you will bite his heel."*
Jesus was the child of the woman because He was born without the
union of a man and He indeed suffered and died on the cross,
crushing and defeating Satan.

Psalm 22 vividly describes Jesus' agonizing death with the first
verse:
> *"My God, my God, why have you left me alone?"*
Isaiah also wrote clearly about Jesus' death on the cross as if he saw
the actual scene:
> *But he was wounded for the wrong things we did. He was
> crushed for the evil things we did. The punishment which
> made us well was given to him. And we are healed because of
> his wounds. We have all wandered away like sheep. Each one
> of us has gone his own way. But the Lord has put on him the
> punishment for all the evil we have done.* (Isaiah 53:5-6)
Other books of the Old Testament also prophesied Jesus would die
for the sin of mankind, from which we see Jesus' death was to be
God's plan for our sin substitute.

When the Roman soldiers and servants of the chief priests and
scribes were arresting Jesus, Jesus told Peter:
> *"Surely you know I could ask my Father, and he would give me
> more than 12 armies of angels. But this thing must happen
> this way so that it will be as the Scriptures say."* (Matthew
> 26:53-54)

As the Word reveals, Jesus' supreme goal was to fulfil God's Word
and do His will rather than care about His own life for the present.
Our Lord Jesus obeyed the Father all the way to death. He did not
save His life because only His death would fulfil the Father's will.

To Save Us

Also, Jesus died to save us. He prayed in Gethsemane:
> *"My Father, if it is possible, do not give me this cup of
> suffering."* (Matthew 26:39)
The cup He was to drink held the deadly poison of all the horrible
and dirty sin and its bondage that mankind had experienced. When
he drank it, God took His face away from Jesus and Jesus cried out:

"My God, my God, why have you left me alone?" (Matthew 27:46)

Why did God turn His face away? Because God could not look upon sin. When the price of sin was paid, Jesus announced to the world, *"It is finished"* (John 19:30). The pressure of the sins of the world, including the price of sins that men would still commit and need forgiveness for down through the centuries of time, were so heavy His body finally broke.

In the Greek language "salvation" is "sozo". "Sozo" means salvation from our real danger, grief and wounds; salvation from sickness, restoring our health; salvation from our spiritual disease that is eternal damnation. The Jesus we believe in is the One Who died on the cross so that we might become healthy and prosper in our lives just as our spirits are quickened.

To Love Us

Another reason for His death on the cross was because His love for us was stronger than His love for His own life. Even while He suffered the pain of crucifixion and the darkness of separation from God He still refused to come down from the cross. If He had come down, we would have had to die for our own sins. The greatest power of His love and willingness to remain on the cross was so that we would not have to die for our sins. Though all the people mocked, criticized and spat on Him, He was a captive of love for us. Such love should make us stand in awe and examine our own hearts to know the degree of our love for Him.

The suffering was beyond our comprehension. Jesus died to obey God, and to save us. He loves us and still does not condemn us for our sins, unrighteousness and ugliness because He already bore and paid for those sins. He patiently waits for us to come to Him. Therefore, we are just to return to Him, confess our sins and accept His shed blood. We are just to acknowledge His work on the cross and give thanks to Him for His suffering, for taking our pain, grief and sorrow and providing full salvation.

Look up to the cross of Jesus! Listen and hear His voice today. He will tell you as you look to Him: "My child, your faults, your sins, your many afflictions have been paid for! Reach out and receive what you need from me and your faith will make you whole."

There has never been one like Jesus in human history. He came among us to walk with us, to commune and have fellowship with us and provide our salvation. He invites us today to come with our needs, extending His nail-scarred hands in love. His body was torn, disfigured and broken for you. He shed all His blood for you. Let us draw near to Him with deep thanksgiving, praise and worship with all of our hearts, for without Him we would not have been able to know sins forgiven or divine health.

CLOSING QUESTIONS

> ### What did the angel of the Lord declare was the purpose of Jesus coming to the world?
> (Matthew 1:21)

> ### How did Jesus manifest God's love?
> (Romans 5:8)

> ### See Isaiah 53:6:
> **a. What did Isaiah liken sinful mankind to?**
> **b. How did the Lord deal with the evil we have done?**

APPLICATION

1. Let us examine our hearts to know whether or not we are totally committed to following Jesus' example of obedience to God unto death.

2. Let us consider what kind of love is the greatest that we can share with others. Let us practise our love in our daily lives.

3. Let us remember again the fact that Jesus died on the cross to pay the penalty for our sins.

JESUS IS RESURRECTED FOR US

1. **Today's Scripture**
   Mark 16:1-18
2. **Memory Verse**
   Mark 16:6
   But the man said, "Don't be afraid. You are looking for Jesus from Nazareth, the one who was killed on a cross. He has risen from death. He is not here. Look, here is the place they laid him."
3. **Reference Scripture**
   1 Corinthians 15:1-11
4. **Objectives**
   a. By studying the proofs of Jesus' resurrection, we can have a more solid faith in Jesus' resurrection.
   b. Let us realize that Jesus' resurrection is for the perfection of salvation.

LEADING QUESTIONS

> ### When was Jesus resurrected?
> (Mark 16:1-2)

> ### What happened to the stone at the tomb when the women arrived there?
> (Mark 16:4)

> ### Who met Jesus first after His resurrection?
> (Mark 16:9)

TODAY'S MESSAGE

The resurrection of Jesus Christ is proof of the life and power of Christianity. With no resurrection Christianity would be a dead religion and our salvation would be vain. Jesus Who died and shed blood to save us, perfected our salvation by rising from the dead. Jesus' resurrection is a fact in history. This lesson will review some prophetic words, some proofs of resurrection throughout the scriptures and also some significant meanings of the resurrection.

Prophecy about the Resurrection

The death of Jesus was real. He did not pretend to be dead, or temporarily faint, like some dared to proclaim. Jesus shed His blood and water when the crown of thorns was plaited and pressed in to His head. The Roman soldiers pierced His side with a spear and He died. Though soldiers broke the legs of the thieves on either side of Jesus, they did not break Jesus' legs because they had confirmed He was already dead. The Jewish people witnessed His death. High priests, the governor Pilate, the women who followed, His disciples, Nicodemus, and Joseph, a rich man from Arimathea, all saw Jesus' death.

But the life of Jesus Christ did not end at the tomb. If Jesus had not been resurrected, our faith would be for nothing as the Apostle Paul said. We would still be guilty of our sins and the dead in Christ would be lost (1 Corinthians 15:17-18). But Jesus *has* risen from the dead. After three days He arose triumphantly, as He had promised, and as the Word of God declared. During his three years on earth, Jesus repeatedly foretold His resurrection:

> *From that time on Jesus began telling his followers that he must go to Jerusalem. He explained that the older Jewish leaders, the leading priests and the teachers of the law would make him suffer many things. And he told them that he must be killed. Then, on the third day, he would be raised from death.* (Matthew 16:21)

He further confirmed His resurrection in John 2:18-22:

> *The Jews said to Jesus, "Show us a miracle for a sign. Prove that you have the right to do these things."*
>
> *Jesus answered, "Destroy this temple, and I will build it again in three days."*
>
> *The Jews answered, "Men worked 46 years to build this Temple! Do you really believe you can build it again in three days?"*
>
> *(But the temple Jesus meant was his own body. After Jesus was raised from death, his followers remembered that Jesus had said this. Then they believed the Scripture and the words Jesus said.)*

Proof of the Resurrection

The resurrection is not a man-made story. All religions speak of the eternity of man's soul, but there has never been a religion that guarantees a resurrection. Man cannot comprehend with his natural mind that he could possibly rise again someday after his death. Resurrection is only possible through God's power, and it can only be known to us through divine revelation from God. Man-made religions cannot possibly teach or promise a resurrection because none of their founders or leaders have been resurrected. But Jesus rose from death as He foretold many times before his crucifixion. There is no room for doubt in His resurrection, because the scripture declares He appeared more than ten times to His disciples, women and crowds.

The Sabbath day passed and as the first rays of dawn broke, Mary Magdalene and other women hurried to the tomb but they could not find the body of Jesus. Instead, an angel spoke:
> "You are looking for Jesus of Nazareth, the one who was killed on a cross. He has risen from death. He is not here."
> (Mark 16:1-8)

After that, some 500 witnesses actually saw the resurrected Jesus for more than 40 days and they even ate together with Him. Thomas, who doubted Jesus' resurrection most, confirmed it was his Lord by seeing Jesus' side and His scarred hands. This tremendous account of the resurrection is not a man-made story. It is a historical fact. Since His resurrection, countless numbers of believers have experienced His resurrection in their lives. Jesus is with us today through the Holy Spirit as He promised:
> "I will continue with you, until the end of the world."
> (Matthew 28:20)

The Meaning of the Resurrection

What are some significant meanings of Jesus' resurrection?

First, the resurrection witnesses that Jesus is truly the Son of God.

If Jesus had not been resurrected, He could not have been more than a mere religionist. His healing of the sick might have been treated as a magical power and His death as the tragic martyrdom of a religious leader. However, because Jesus arose, His word and teachings were confirmed to be God's Word, His healings were confirmed to be healing from God and His death to be the redemptive sacrifice for man's sin. The resurrection of Jesus witnessed once and for all that Jesus is the Son of God.

Second, the resurrection of Jesus guarantees that our sins are forgiven, and that is our salvation. If Jesus had remained buried in the tomb, we would still have remained in sin.

Since the purpose of Jesus dying on the cross was to become the sacrifice offering for all man's sins, if He had not been resurrected, it means the price would not have been paid for our sins. But He was resurrected! Consequently, the price of all of our sins has been paid and we have become free persons through His death and resurrection.

Third, the resurrection of Jesus is proof of our future resurrection to come.

> *It is preached that Christ was raised from death. So why do some of you say that people will not be raised from death? If no one will ever be raised from death, then Christ was not raised from death.* (1 Corinthians 15:12-13)

Fourth, Jesus' resurrection gives us daily strength to overcome the obstacles of our present life, because through the power of His resurrection Jesus defeated sin, death and the devil. Also the hope of our forthcoming resurrection leads us daily to victory over sin and the devil.

As we shared above, the resurrection of Jesus is evidence that Jesus is God's Son; that He purchased the deed for our salvation; that as He was resurrected so we will be resurrected too; and that because of Jesus' resurrection we have the power to change despair to hope and adversity to blessing every day.

CLOSING QUESTIONS

> ### What did Jesus say would happen after His death?
> (John 2:19-22)

> ### What did the apostles repeatedly witness about?
> (Acts 3:14-15; 4:33)

> ### What was Jesus appointed to be by His resurrection?
> (Romans 1:4)

Now consider the application of this lesson which you will find on the next page.

APPLICATION

1. A believer should always know that "Jesus' death is my death and His resurrection is my resurrection" and "I died with Jesus on the cross and I am resurrected with Him from the grave of my past". Let us search our hearts – "Did I really mortify my lust and greed on the cross and am I really resurrected with Christ?"

2. Let us start each day by confessing: "Living in Jesus' resurrection will lead to victory again today."

JESUS WILL RETURN FOR US

1. **Today's Scripture**
   Acts 1:1-11
2. **Memory Verse**
   Acts 1:11
   > *They said, "Men of Galilee, why are you standing here looking into the sky? You saw Jesus taken away from you into heaven. He will come back in the same way you saw him go."*
3. **Reference Scripture**
   Mark 16:19-20
   Luke 24:50-53
4. **Objectives**
   a. Let us realize that Jesus sent us the Holy Spirit for our sake because He ascended to heaven.
   b. Let us firmly believe that Jesus Who ascended will return in the same way as He ascended.
   c. Let us always prepare for Jesus' return by watching, living and praying diligently.

LEADING QUESTIONS

> ### How long did Jesus stay in this world after He was resurrected?
> (Acts 1:3)

> ### What were His last words before He ascended?
> (Acts 1:8)

> ### What did the angels say to the disciples who were looking up as Jesus was taken up into a cloud?
> (Acts 1:11)

TODAY'S MESSAGE

Jesus was resurrected and stayed on earth with His disciples for about 40 days and then ascended back to His Father. As He ascended to His Father, Jesus promised His disciples He would return just as they saw Him depart. This promise had been made by Jesus several times when He taught the disciples about the end time. These days we, too, find Jesus' prophecies are being fulfilled one by one.

This lesson will review several points such as Christ's second advent, prophecies in the Bible about the end time, those prophecies already fulfilled that have been spoken through Daniel, and the status of the end-time church.

Historical Prophecy and the End Time

600 years before Jesus Christ was born, King Nebuchadnezzar of Babylon had a dream:

> *"My king, in your dream you saw a large statue in front of you. It was huge, shiny and frightening. The head of the statue was made of pure gold. Its chest and arms were made of silver. Its middle and the upper part of its legs were made of bronze. The lower part of the legs were made of iron. Its feet were made partly of iron and partly of baked clay. While you were looking at the statue, you saw a rock cut free. But no human being touched the rock. It hit the statue on its feet of iron and clay and smashed them. Then the iron, clay, bronze, silver and gold broke to pieces at the same time. They became like chaff on a threshing floor in the summertime. The wind blew them away, and there was nothing left. Then the rock that hit the statue became a very large mountain. It filled the whole earth."* (Daniel 2:31-35)

This dream outlines the spread of world history after fall of the "head of pure gold", or Babylon. The "chest and arms of silver" were interpreted as Media and Persia; the "bronze middle" as Macedonia's King Alexander, the bronze thighs as the era of the Roman empire, which links to ten toes. The ten toes represent ten European countries today.

When the end of world history arrives, the European common countries will number ten and these ten countries will be united and replay the power of the old Roman empire. When they become united into one state, a "stone" cut out without hands will come down from heaven, that is Jesus Christ.

> *Because of these things, this is what the Lord God says: "I will put a stone in the ground in Jerusalem. This will be a tested stone. Everything will be built on this important and precious rock. Anyone who trusts in it will never be disappointed."* (Isaiah 28:16)

Returning to earth and striking the countries which make up the "ten toes", Jesus Christ will bring world history to an end. As the stone in King Nebuchadnezzar's dream filled the whole earth, the kingdom of Jesus Christ, the eternal heavenly kingdom, will fill the earth.

In the latter part of Daniel's prophecy facts about the end time are more detailed. Antichrist will come out of the ten united European states and will conquer three countries and gradually seven others. They will rebel against God gradually. God will then take antichrist and cast him into the lake of fire and brimstone together with his followers. The second advent of Messiah will then take place. Jesus will rule the earth with power and glory!

Actual Fulfilment of Daniel's Prophecy

The Bible speaks of the independence of the country of Israel as a very prominent sign of the end time:
> *"The fig tree teaches us a lesson: When its branches become green and soft, and new leaves begin to grow, then you know that summer is near. So also when you see all these things happening, you will know that the time is near, ready to come."* (Matthew 24:32-33)

As the Word of God foretold: the fig tree which we interpreted as Israel became independent in 1948 and the ten horns, the European common countries, are now in the process of becoming more solidly united.

The antichrist, a leader-figure from these united European countries, will be elected and he will make a seven-year covenant with Israel to help build Jehovah's temple on Mount Zion.

For three and a half years the people of Israel will welcome as their Messiah, this man who helped build their temple. After the three and a half years have passed, Satan, who was defeated in the war in the heavens, will enter the antichrist so that he will be able to force Israel to worship idols. Those who refuse to worship the idols will be ruthlessly slaughtered. Except for those chosen Jews which the Bible says will be saved, all Jews will be murdered during that period.

During another three and a half years, an army of possibly 200 million will attack the antichrist. In Armageddon, Palestine, the most horrible war in human history will begin, resulting in human blood flowing up to the horse's bridle. Then our Saviour and Lord Jesus will return to earth on a white horse together with His saints. The antichrist will be cast into the lake of fire and brimstone and the unbelievers will be judged. Jesus' millennial Kingdom will be established.

Those who accepted Jesus' sacrifice and redemption for their sins on the cross, the true Body of Christ, will not be judged again. Therefore before this seven years of tribulation begins (and the seven-year covenant with Israel is made) the church will be raptured to meet Jesus in the clouds. The church will not pass through the seven-year period of tribulation.

The Churches in the End Time

The Bible tells that as the end time draws near many will depart from the faith and go back into the world. Today countless people are following spirits of error and doctrines of devils. Many do not realize that they have been seduced. New theologians deny Jesus' virgin birth, the presence of heaven and a real hell. They claim true Christianity is only social reformation. Born out of this social reformation are some elements of error that climax with the teaching that if everyone were to eat equally well, dress well and live in the best homes, that would be true Christianity. Other groups hear devils' voices and claim that they are Messiahs, or special prophets for today.

In this turmoil, we must hold fast to our faith in Jesus Who is the Way, the Truth and the Life. In James 5:7, the Bible gives a picture of the latter days:

> Brothers, be patient until the Lord comes again. A farmer is patient. He waits for his valuable crop to grow from the earth. He waits patiently for it to receive the first rain and the last rain. You, too, must be patient. Do not give up hope. The Lord is coming soon.

Our Lord Jesus Christ is preparing His bride, those who love Jesus, through many fiery tests and by the power of the Holy Spirit, so that He can take them unto Himself.

People today think the end time is still far away but history provides evidence that it is very near. In Bible terms, we are living now in the era of "adornment" by the Holy Spirit, who is preparing us to be raptured. Let us be awakened in our prayer life. Let us live in earnest expectation of Jesus' return. If the Holy Spirit prods us to take care of sins in our lives, be they large or small, let us run to the "Light" and ask Jesus to expose them to us, cleanse us again with His precious blood and make us ready for the rapture.

CLOSING QUESTIONS

> **What is Jesus doing now for all of us while He is seated at the right hand of God?**
> (Romans 8:34)

> **What is meant by "the fig tree .... becomes green and soft and new leaves begin to grow"?**
> (Matthew 24:32-33)

> **How does the Bible explain the things of antichrist?**
> (Daniel 9:27)

> **Believing that we are living in the end time, what should we stop doing and what should we take up?**
> (Romans 13:11-24)

APPLICATION

1. Seeing the end time is upon us, let us become more sober than ever, revere God's Word more, and meditate on His Word.

2. Let us discuss together how the Bible prophecies of the end time are specifically being fulfilled these days.

3. Just like the wise virgins who were prepared with oil in their lamps, let us also be prepared daily and never become lazy. Let us diligently read the Word and pray so that we will be prepared for His coming.

JESUS STILL CONTINUES HIS
MINISTRY

1. **Today's Scripture**
   John 16:7-15
2. **Memory Verse**
   John 16:13
   "But when the Spirit of truth comes he will lead you into all truth. He will not speak his own words. He will speak only what he hears and will tell you what is to come."
3. **Reference Scripture**
   Acts 2:1-4
   John 14:16
4. **Objectives**
   a. Let us know our Lord Jesus Who, resurrected and ascended, is still alive and continues His work among us through the Holy Spirit.
   b. Let us never become such believers as hinder or resist the work of the Holy Spirit.

LEADING QUESTIONS

> **According to the scripture, what benefit would Jesus' departure render to the disciples?**
> (John 16:7)

> **What is the work of the Holy Spirit?**
> (John 16:8)

> **What does the Holy Spirit speak to us about?**
> (John 16:13)

TODAY'S MESSAGE

Before His ascension Jesus made an awesome promise to us: *"So go and make followers of all people in the world. Baptize them in the name of the Father and the Son and the Holy Spirit. Teach them to obey everything that I have told you. You can be sure that I will be with you always. I will continue with you until the end of the world."* (Matthew 29:19-20)

".... if two or three come together in my name, I am there with them." (Matthew 18:20)

How can Jesus, Who has ascended in His resurrected body, still be with us until the end of the world? This lesson will review how Jesus can be with us and how His present ministry can continue through the Holy Spirit.

The Other Comforter that Jesus Promised

Jesus said, in John 14:16 (AV):
> *"And I will pray the Father, and he shall give you another Comforter, that he may abide with you for ever."*

Jesus, as the first Comforter (Helper EB), came in human flesh to mankind and granted help to many people of that time, those who were hurting spiritually, mentally and physically. The help He rendered was complete, that is full salvation for us.

When this first Comforter, Jesus, ascended to Heaven, His followers fell into great consternation, but Jesus told His bewildered disciples that He would not leave them like orphans. He would send another Comforter. Here "another" means, in the Greek, "allos", which is used to indicate "another of the same kind". For example, when two of the same kind of product came out of a factory line, each of the goods may be called "allos" or "two of a kind". Jesus, the first Comforter, and the Holy Spirit (another Comforter), are not different from each other. They are two of the same kind of Persons. After Jesus ascended, the Holy Spirit, as another Comforter, descended to continue Jesus' ministry. The work of the Holy Spirit is the work of Jesus and the presence of the Holy Spirit is the presence of Jesus.

Likewise, as the bodily resurrected Jesus sits at the right hand of God's throne, another Comforter like Him, the Holy Spirit, is among us and continues the same work that Jesus began to do. The coming of the Holy Spirit is the same as Jesus' coming to us and so consequently we are not left as orphans.

The Ministry of the Holy Spirit

The "other Comforter" our Lord sent for us does the exact same work as Jesus did. The Holy Spirit convicts of sin, heals the sick, casts devils out, changes death to life, and changes despair to joy and hope. The Holy Spirit who descended into Mark's upper room on the day of Pentecost is embracing us just as air surrounds the air and water. The Holy Spirit is working beside us always. The Holy Spirit Who is with us prevents the waves of sin from engulfing us. He delivers us from the devil's oppression. He reproaches sins in our lives that are unconfessed. He shows us our need for righteousness and He judges sin. So the Holy Spirit leads us to repent and believe in Jesus. He does not tolerate sin but reproves and convicts us of sin.

When we came to Jesus and confessed our sins, it was the Holy Spirit Who led us to Jesus, and now He is with us reminding us of the benefits of Jesus' blood, to keep us from sinning when we are tempted and to continue to cleanse when necessary. As we believe in Jesus as our Saviour and Lord, the Holy Spirit leads us day by day.

Also, when we earnestly pray, the Holy Spirit gives us power: power to pray, power to win souls, power to believe, and power to lead a victorious life every day.

The Holy Spirit is with us, is over us, surrounds us, and He will be with us eternally. He enables us to experience all that Jesus purchased for us and to enjoy it eternally.

Attitudes that Hinder the Work of the Holy Spirit

Today Jesus Christ works through the Holy Spirit; however, if there are wrong attitudes in our hearts they will hinder Him from working. What are the hindering attitudes that prevent the Holy Spirit's work?

First, **hatred** in the heart hinders the work of the Holy Spirit. A hate-filled heart is the work of the devil. If we permit the devil to come into our hearts, through bitter thoughts and attitudes, we must cast out the hatred in the name of Jesus. Instead of hating someone who does wrong to us, we must bless our enemies, as Jesus instructs us, and the Holy Spirit will work in us.

The second hindrance to the work of the Holy Spirit is a **fearful** heart. Those who are trembling in insecurity and fear cannot believe in Jesus. They cannot pray to Him and cannot enjoy the grace and blessing from our Heavenly Father. When insecurity and fear are trying to invade our hearts, we must cast them out in the name of Jesus. We must rely on the Holy Spirit to bring the love and faith of our Lord Jesus to occupy our hearts and let love and faith flow and overflow in us.

The third hindrance to the work of the Holy Spirit is an **inferiority complex**. Those who allow an inferiority complex to rule their hearts will find the Holy Spirit cannot work either. God purchased us with the precious blood of Jesus. Consequently, we are God's children. We have become kingly priests. We are declared righteous enough to receive blessings from Him. We must dwell on this rather than dwell on being unworthy. In prayer we must cast out any inferiority complex in Jesus' name so the Holy Spirit can work in us and we can enjoy God's blessings.

The fourth hindrance to the work of the Holy Spirit is a **guilt complex**. If we allow this to rule our hearts, our faith in Jesus and the work of the Holy Spirit will come to a temporary halt. We must repent of our sins to Jesus, receive His forgiveness, forgive ourselves and then cast out the guilt complex.

We must look into our hearts and if hatred, fear, an inferiority complex, or a guilt complex is there, we must cast it out. When we do so, the Holy Spirit will sweep over us like the waves of a sea and occupy our hearts.

In Jesus Christ, we possess new hope, new faith and new love. We can become winners! We can experience miracles! We are blessed children of God because Jesus died on the cross and was resurrected so that we could be forgiven, healed and delivered from death.

The Holy Spirit is with us just now to impart everything that Jesus died for. The Holy Spirit wants to help us cast out any or all of these hindering forces that would keep us from enjoying God's full grace and blessings.

CLOSING QUESTIONS

> ### Jesus said that through the Holy Spirit He would not leave us like what?
> (John 14:18)

> ### In Romans 8:26, the "other Comforter", the Holy Spirit, also helps us especially in what area?

> ### What law delivered us from the law of sin and death?
> (Romans 8:2)

Now consider the application of this lesson which you will find on the next page.

APPLICATION

1. In our daily lives, let us welcome the Holy Spirit, acknowledge Him, trust Him and love Him and we will experience all He wants to do for us.

2. Let us pray together when any of our homecell members or Christian friends are in trouble, so that the work of the Holy Spirit will be clearly shown.

PRAYER: KEY TO REVIVAL
Dr. Paul Y. Cho

Published in March 1985 and reprinted six times in the same year, this best-selling title has now been reissued with a 32 page study guide. Dr. Cho says, 'It is because I believe in revival and renewal that I have written this book. It has been historically true that prayer has been the key to every revival in the history of Christianity.'

From his experience as a pastor, Dr. Cho answers general questions such as *why* to pray and *when* to pray. He also deals with specific queries like, 'What does prayer accomplish?' 'What part does the Holy Spirit play in prayer?' and 'Why does fasting increase the effectiveness of prayer?'

His study is based on one simple premise: 'God has no favourite children . . . If God has worked through men and women in the past, He can work through you.'

'This is the best book I have ever read on prayer.'
EVANGELISM TODAY

DR. PAUL CHO, who was converted from Buddhism as a young man, is now Pastor of the Central Church in Seoul, which has grown to over half a million members. He is also founder of Church Growth International.

Catalogue Number YB 9059 £2.75

MORE THAN NUMBERS
Dr. Paul Y. Cho

No one is better qualified to speak out on the sometimes misunderstood church growth movement than Dr. Cho. A pastor with over thirty years' experience, he now leads a church in Seoul, Korea, which currently has over a million members. He writes, however, that 'Success has not come quickly or easily. Most of the lessons I have learned have come as a result of passing difficult tests in my life and ministry.'

Dr. Cho writes with a theological sensitivity which enables him to base church growth on a solid spiritual foundation instead of mere technique, discussing such diverse topics as revival, the cell system, the media and the Kingdom of God.

'Word Books have done the church a service by reissuing this excellent book by Dr. Cho. I regard it as vital reading on church growth. There is nothing stereotyped about Cho's teaching – he is a man of the Spirit and this comes through clearly.'

COLIN WHITTAKER, RENEWAL

Catalogue Number YB 9100   £2.25

PRAYING WITH JESUS
Dr. Paul Y. Cho

Prayer is a dialogue with God in which our attitudes and thoughts are grafted into God's thoughts.

In *Praying with Jesus* the author takes us deep into the teaching of the Lord's Prayer. This is the perfect model for our own prayers but more than that, it shows us how to align our thoughts with God's purposes for the world and for His people.

For prayer to be accomplished our thoughts on God must be right, and this is where the book begins. Dr. Cho then takes us phrase by phrase through the rest of the Lord's Prayer. He writes not only with theological insight, but as a pastor who has seen these principles working out in people's lives over the years.

If you want to receive clearer answers to your prayers, if you simply want to draw nearer to God, then try *Praying with Jesus*.

Catalogue Number YB 9165 £2.50